Blueprints for the Cloud: Architecting on Azure

First Edition

Preface

Cloud architecture is rapidly reshaping the way organizations think about infrastructure, scalability, and digital transformation. The dynamic nature of the cloud ecosystem—especially on platforms like Microsoft Azure—requires a foundational yet forward-thinking approach to design, deployment, and maintenance. This book, *Blueprints for the Cloud: Architecting on Azure*, serves as a practical introduction to the principles, services, and patterns essential for anyone embarking on a journey into cloud architecture with Azure.

Unlike traditional cloud books that tend to get lost in theory or overburden with exhaustive configuration steps, this guide aims to hit the sweet spot between conceptual clarity and real-world application. It's been crafted specifically for architects, developers, IT professionals, and students who want to understand *how* to think about cloud systems, *why* certain design decisions are made, and *what* tools Azure provides to make those designs a reality.

Chapter 1 lays the foundation by walking through core cloud paradigms and how Azure fits into the broader cloud ecosystem. You'll understand the shift from traditional to modern architecture and the importance of cloud-native thinking.

Chapter 2 introduces the primary Azure services you'll use in nearly every architectural pattern—from compute to networking to monitoring. The goal here is to build familiarity and confidence with Azure's toolbox.

In Chapter 3, we dig into performance and scalability. You'll explore the architectural strategies and Azure-specific capabilities that help systems scale seamlessly and perform under variable load.

Resilience and high availability are critical themes in Chapter 4. Here, we focus on redundancy, failover strategies, and how Azure's global infrastructure can be used to design fault-tolerant systems.

Security is baked into every level of a successful architecture. Chapter 5 unpacks Azure's security services and practices, emphasizing proactive security through identity, encryption, and compliance.

In Chapter 6, we pivot to application design, diving into multi-tier models, microservices, APIs, and event-driven systems using Azure-native tools like AKS, Service Fabric, and Service Bus.

Chapter 7 explores DevOps culture and automation. You'll learn how to codify your infrastructure with Bicep and Terraform, deploy via pipelines, and monitor rollouts to mitigate risk.

Cost management often goes overlooked, but Chapter 8 ensures that doesn't happen to you. It outlines how to design with cost in mind, estimate spend, and use Azure's budgeting tools to avoid surprises.

To ground your learning, Chapter 9 presents reference architectures and case studies drawn from real-world Azure implementations. These examples give context and inspiration for your own projects.

Chapter 10 peers into the future, examining trends like serverless, edge computing, and quantum services—ensuring that your foundational knowledge is adaptable to tomorrow's innovations.

Finally, Chapter 11 includes valuable appendices with glossaries, sample projects, code snippets, and other resources to support continued learning.

Whether you're brand new to Azure or brushing up your skills, this book is designed to serve as your reliable companion through the cloud architecture journey. Welcome aboard.

Table of Contents

Chapter 1: Introduction to Cloud Architecture

Understanding Cloud Computing Paradigms

Cloud computing represents a transformative shift in how individuals and enterprises consume, deploy, and think about IT infrastructure. Rather than relying solely on physical hardware managed in-house, cloud computing enables on-demand access to compute, storage, networking, and application services over the internet. But to truly understand the essence of cloud computing—and how Azure fits into this paradigm—it's vital to examine the models that define the cloud landscape.

Cloud Delivery Models

There are three primary cloud service models, each serving different needs and levels of abstraction:

- **Infrastructure as a Service (IaaS)**
  IaaS provides virtualized computing resources over the internet. In this model, users rent servers, storage, and networking infrastructure from the cloud provider and are responsible for managing the operating system, applications, and data.
  Examples: Azure Virtual Machines, Azure Load Balancer, Azure Blob Storage.

- **Platform as a Service (PaaS)**
  PaaS abstracts much of the infrastructure management away, allowing developers to focus on application logic and functionality. Azure handles the underlying OS, servers, and runtime environments.
  Examples: Azure App Service, Azure Functions, Azure SQL Database.

- **Software as a Service (SaaS)**
  SaaS provides complete, ready-to-use applications over the internet. Users don't worry about infrastructure or platforms—everything is managed by the provider.
  Examples: Microsoft 365, Dynamics 365, Azure DevOps Boards.

These models aren't mutually exclusive. Many architectures blend elements of all three, depending on the business requirements.

Deployment Models

Cloud deployment models define how cloud services are made available. Azure supports several, each offering different levels of control, scalability, and privacy:

- **Public Cloud**
  Services are delivered over the internet and shared among multiple tenants. Azure

operates under this model as a hyperscale public cloud provider.

- **Private**   **Cloud**
  Infrastructure is provisioned for a single organization, either on-premises or hosted by a third party. Azure Stack enables private cloud deployments using Azure's tools and APIs.

- **Hybrid**   **Cloud**
  Combines public and private clouds, allowing data and applications to be shared between them. Hybrid setups are ideal for regulatory compliance, data residency, or gradual   migration.

- **Multicloud**
  A strategy involving the use of services from multiple cloud providers (e.g., Azure and AWS) to avoid vendor lock-in or optimize performance across regions.

Each deployment model has unique trade-offs in terms of cost, control, and complexity, and must be aligned with the organization's strategic goals.

The Shift from Traditional to Cloud-Native

Before the cloud, infrastructure was monolithic, static, and often overprovisioned to account for peak usage. It could take weeks to acquire hardware and deploy new environments. Cloud computing has turned this model on its head. Now, resources are:

- **Elastic**:   They   scale   dynamically   based   on   demand.

- **On-demand**:   They   can   be   provisioned   or   deprovisioned   in   seconds.

- **Programmatic**: Infrastructure can be managed with code (Infrastructure as Code, or IaC).

- **Globally Available**: Services span regions and availability zones, reducing latency and   improving   redundancy.

This shift has also enabled a new design mindset known as **cloud-native architecture**. Instead of "lifting and shifting" traditional systems into the cloud, cloud-native systems are:

- **Resilient**:   Built   to   fail   gracefully.

- **Scalable**:   Designed   to   handle   variable   workloads.

- **Observable**: Expose internal states through metrics, logs, and traces.

- **Automated**: Use CI/CD pipelines for frequent, reliable deployments.

Here's a simple representation of IaC using Terraform for provisioning an Azure Virtual Machine:

```
provider "azurerm" {
  features {}
}

resource "azurerm_resource_group" "example" {
  name     = "myResourceGroup"
  location = "East US"
}

resource "azurerm_virtual_network" "example" {
  name                = "myVnet"
  address_space       = ["10.0.0.0/16"]
  location            = azurerm_resource_group.example.location
  resource_group_name = azurerm_resource_group.example.name
}

resource "azurerm_subnet" "example" {
  name                 = "mySubnet"
  resource_group_name  = azurerm_resource_group.example.name
  virtual_network_name = azurerm_virtual_network.example.name
  address_prefixes     = ["10.0.1.0/24"]
}
```

This code declares your infrastructure in a way that's version-controlled, repeatable, and automated.

Benefits and Challenges of the Cloud

Benefits:

- **Reduced Capital Expenditure**: No need for upfront hardware purchases.

- **Increased Agility**: Faster provisioning means faster time-to-market.

- **Global Reach**: Deploy workloads close to users around the world.

- **Built-In Security**: Azure provides advanced security features by default.

- **Disaster Recovery**: Geographic redundancy makes recovery faster and more reliable.

Challenges:

- **Vendor Lock-In**: Proprietary APIs and services can make migration costly.

- **Learning Curve**: The pace of innovation can be overwhelming.

- **Cost Management**: Without proper governance, costs can spiral.

- **Latency and Bandwidth**: Network dependency can affect performance.

Organizations must weigh these pros and cons when choosing to migrate or build on the cloud.

Conclusion

Understanding cloud computing paradigms is essential to becoming a proficient cloud architect. Azure provides the tools and frameworks necessary to implement each of these paradigms, from IaaS to PaaS to SaaS, and across all deployment models. Whether you're creating a global SaaS product, migrating legacy apps, or designing a hybrid solution, your architectural decisions should always be grounded in a clear understanding of these foundational concepts. In the chapters that follow, we'll apply this knowledge to real-world use cases and examine how Azure helps you turn ideas into scalable, resilient, and secure systems.

The Evolution of Cloud Architecture

Cloud architecture has undergone a significant transformation over the past two decades, driven by changes in technology, business needs, and user expectations. Understanding this evolution is critical for cloud architects, as it helps contextualize modern design patterns, highlights the motivations behind them, and enables informed decision-making when working with platforms like Microsoft Azure.

From Data Centers to Virtualization

Before the rise of cloud computing, IT infrastructure was grounded in physical data centers. Enterprises would invest in costly hardware, install operating systems manually, and provision applications on dedicated servers. This model, often referred to as **on-premises architecture**, was characterized by several inefficiencies:

- **Underutilization**: Servers ran at low capacity most of the time.

- **Long Procurement Cycles**: Hardware acquisition and provisioning took weeks or months.

- **Lack of Agility**: Scaling required physical upgrades.

- **Operational Overhead**: IT teams managed everything from cooling to firmware updates.

The advent of **virtualization** in the early 2000s was a major turning point. Tools like VMware and Microsoft Hyper-V allowed multiple virtual machines (VMs) to run on a single physical server, drastically improving hardware utilization and flexibility. This gave birth to **private clouds**, where enterprises could manage virtualized resources internally with greater agility.

However, private cloud still required significant capital investment and in-house expertise. This limitation laid the groundwork for **public cloud computing**—offering computing resources as a utility, similar to electricity or water.

The Rise of Public Cloud Platforms

In the mid-2000s, companies like Amazon (with AWS), Google, and Microsoft introduced public cloud platforms. Microsoft Azure launched in 2010, positioning itself as a flexible, enterprise-friendly platform built on the strength of Microsoft's software ecosystem.

Public cloud platforms provided on-demand access to compute, storage, and network services. Key breakthroughs included:

- **Elasticity**: Resources could scale automatically based on demand.

- **Pay-as-you-go**: Costs were tied to actual usage, not fixed hardware.

- **Global Reach**: Cloud regions and availability zones enabled low-latency access for global   users.

- **Service Abstraction**: Users could consume services without needing to manage the underlying   infrastructure.

This democratized access to computing power and fueled innovations across startups, enterprises, and government agencies.

Generations of Cloud Architecture

As cloud computing matured, architectural patterns evolved through several distinct generations:

First Generation: Lift-and-Shift (IaaS-Centric)

In the early days of cloud adoption, most organizations used a **lift-and-shift** approach— migrating on-premises applications and workloads to cloud-based virtual machines.

Characteristics:

- Direct replication of existing architecture
- Minimal changes to application code
- Focus on IaaS (e.g., Azure Virtual Machines, Azure Load Balancer)
- Fast migration but limited optimization

While this method provided immediate benefits in terms of cost and availability, it often failed to leverage the full potential of the cloud.

Second Generation: Cloud-Optimized (PaaS Emphasis)

Next came **cloud-optimized** architectures. Applications were restructured to take advantage of PaaS offerings and managed services.

Key services in Azure:

- **Azure App Service**: For web applications and REST APIs
- **Azure SQL Database**: A fully managed relational database
- **Azure Functions**: Serverless compute for event-driven apps

Benefits included auto-scaling, built-in monitoring, reduced operational overhead, and better cost control.

Here's an example of defining an Azure Function in C#:

```
public static class HelloWorldFunction
{
    [FunctionName("HelloWorld")]
    public static IActionResult Run(
        [HttpTrigger(AuthorizationLevel.Anonymous,    "get",    "post",
Route = null)] HttpRequest req,
        ILogger log)
    {
        log.LogInformation("Processing request.");
        return new OkObjectResult("Hello from Azure Functions!");
    }
}
```

This snippet illustrates how a few lines of code can define a serverless HTTP endpoint without provisioning infrastructure.

Third Generation: Cloud-Native (Microservices and Containers)

The third generation represents a major shift toward **cloud-native architecture**, characterized by:

- **Microservices**: Small, independently deployable services

- **Containers**: Lightweight, portable runtime environments

- **Service Meshes**: For inter-service communication

- **CI/CD Pipelines**: Automated integration and delivery

- **DevOps Culture**: Collaboration between development and operations

Azure supports cloud-native development through:

- **Azure Kubernetes Service (AKS)**: Managed Kubernetes

- **Azure Container Registry (ACR)**: Private container storage

- **Dapr**: A runtime for building microservices

In this model, applications are decomposed into modular services that communicate over APIs or message queues.

Here's a Dockerfile to containerize a .NET web API:

```
FROM mcr.microsoft.com/dotnet/aspnet:6.0 AS base
WORKDIR /app
EXPOSE 80

FROM mcr.microsoft.com/dotnet/sdk:6.0 AS build
WORKDIR /src
COPY ["MyApp/MyApp.csproj", "MyApp/"]
RUN dotnet restore "MyApp/MyApp.csproj"
COPY . .
WORKDIR "/src/MyApp"
RUN dotnet build "MyApp.csproj" -c Release -o /app/build

FROM build AS publish
RUN dotnet publish "MyApp.csproj" -c Release -o /app/publish

FROM base AS final
```

```
WORKDIR /app
COPY --from=publish /app/publish .
ENTRYPOINT ["dotnet", "MyApp.dll"]
```

This approach embraces modularity, continuous delivery, and scalability.

Fourth Generation: Serverless and Event-Driven

Modern applications increasingly use **serverless computing** and **event-driven architectures** to improve agility and reduce operational complexity.

Azure enables this model through:

- **Azure Event Grid**: Reactive event routing
- **Azure Service Bus**: Enterprise-grade messaging
- **Azure Logic Apps**: Workflow automation
- **Durable Functions**: Stateful workflows in serverless applications

Use cases include IoT event ingestion, real-time analytics, and workflow orchestration. These systems are highly responsive, loosely coupled, and scalable.

Here's a basic Logic App workflow definition:

```json
{
  "definition": {
    "$schema":
"https://schema.management.azure.com/providers/Microsoft.Logic/schem
as/2016-06-01/workflowdefinition.json#",
    "actions": {
      "Send_email": {
        "type": "ApiConnection",
        "inputs": {
          "host": {
            "connection": {
              "name":
"@parameters('$connections')['office365']['connectionId']"
            }
          },
          "method": "post",
          "path": "/v2/Mail",
          "body": {
```

```
            "Subject": "Alert",
            "To": "admin@example.com",
            "Body": "An event has occurred."
          }
        }
      }
    },
    "triggers": {
      "manual": {
        "type": "Request",
        "kind": "Http",
        "inputs": {
          "schema": {}
        }
      }
    }
  }
}
```

Serverless architecture reduces TCO and operational effort, enabling teams to focus purely on business logic.

Industry Adoption and Enterprise Trends

Today, enterprises are accelerating digital transformation through:

- **Cloud-first strategies**: All new workloads are deployed to the cloud.

- **Hybrid cloud**: Leveraging both on-prem and cloud for compliance and flexibility.

- **Multicloud**: Distributing workloads across multiple providers (Azure, AWS, GCP).

- **Zero Trust Security**: Treating every access request as untrusted until verified.

Microsoft Azure has become a preferred platform for regulated industries due to its compliance certifications, hybrid tooling (Azure Arc, Azure Stack), and integration with Microsoft 365 and Active Directory.

Cloud Architecture Maturity Models

Organizations often progress through stages of cloud maturity:

1. **Ad Hoc**: Minimal cloud usage, isolated workloads.

2. **Opportunistic**: Experimentation with PaaS and serverless.

3. **Systematic**: Standardization, centralized governance, and automation.

4. **Transformational**: Business-driven innovation, DevSecOps, and continuous optimization.

Azure's native tools support each maturity level:

- **Azure Blueprints**: For enforcing governance

- **Azure Policy**: For compliance

- **Azure DevOps and GitHub Actions**: For DevOps

- **Azure Monitor and Log Analytics**: For observability

Conclusion

The evolution of cloud architecture—from physical servers to serverless computing—reflects a broader shift in how software is designed, deployed, and operated. Each generation built on the last, increasing abstraction, automation, and agility.

Microsoft Azure, as a comprehensive cloud platform, supports this evolution with a rich ecosystem of services across IaaS, PaaS, and SaaS. Whether migrating legacy apps or building greenfield solutions, understanding the trajectory of cloud architecture allows architects to make better decisions and deliver scalable, secure, and resilient systems.

In the next section, we'll explore why Azure has become a go-to platform for cloud architects and how its unique offerings compare to other cloud providers.

Why Azure? A Platform Overview

As cloud computing has become the backbone of modern digital infrastructure, organizations face a multitude of choices when selecting a cloud platform. Among the industry leaders—Amazon Web Services (AWS), Google Cloud Platform (GCP), and Microsoft Azure—Azure has emerged as a compelling option for businesses of all sizes, particularly those in regulated, enterprise, or hybrid environments.

This section delves into what makes Azure unique, how its services align with real-world architectural needs, and why it is often chosen as the foundational platform for digital transformation.

Strategic Positioning and Enterprise Adoption

Microsoft Azure benefits from Microsoft's longstanding relationships with enterprises, educational institutions, and governments. Organizations already invested in Windows Server, SQL Server, Active Directory, and Microsoft 365 often find Azure to be a natural extension of their IT infrastructure.

Key factors contributing to Azure's widespread enterprise adoption include:

- **Integration with Microsoft Ecosystem**: Azure tightly integrates with tools like Visual Studio, Power BI, Dynamics 365, and Microsoft Defender.

- **Enterprise Agreements and Licensing**: Existing Microsoft licensing agreements often reduce Azure costs via hybrid benefits.

- **Global Reach**: Azure operates in more than 60 regions worldwide—more than any other cloud provider.

- **Compliance and Security**: Azure supports over 100 compliance certifications, including HIPAA, FedRAMP, ISO 27001, and GDPR.

Azure Global Infrastructure

Azure's infrastructure is designed to deliver high availability, fault tolerance, and global scalability. This is achieved through:

- **Regions**: Geographically distributed data centers grouped by location (e.g., West Europe, East US).

- **Availability Zones**: Physically separate data centers within a region, offering redundancy.

- **Edge Zones**: Local extensions of Azure's cloud, enabling low-latency access for edge computing use cases.

- **Sovereign Clouds**: Specialized instances of Azure for government use (e.g., Azure Government, Azure China).

Here's an example of deploying a resource group in a specific region using Azure CLI:

```
az group create --name dev-rg --location "East US"
```

This command creates a resource group in Azure's East US region, demonstrating how developers can choose regions based on compliance or latency needs.

Service Categories and Capabilities

Azure offers a comprehensive portfolio of services spanning every major area of cloud computing. These are grouped into several key categories:

Compute

Azure provides a variety of compute services for different architectural needs:

- **Azure Virtual Machines**: IaaS offering for running Windows or Linux VMs.

- **App Service**: PaaS for web apps, REST APIs, and mobile backends.

- **Azure Functions**: Serverless compute for event-driven tasks.

- **Azure Kubernetes Service (AKS)**: Managed Kubernetes clusters for microservices and container orchestration.

- **Azure Container Instances (ACI)**: Lightweight container deployment without orchestration overhead.

Use case example—Deploying a basic Azure Function using the Azure Functions Core Tools:

```
func init MyFunctionProj --worker-runtime dotnet
cd MyFunctionProj
func new --name HelloWorld --template "HTTP trigger"
func start
```

This illustrates how quickly serverless compute can be set up locally and deployed to Azure.

Storage

Azure storage is built for durability, scalability, and security:

- **Blob Storage**: Object storage for unstructured data (e.g., media, backups).

- **File Storage**: SMB-based file shares for lift-and-shift scenarios.

- **Queue Storage**: Message queueing for decoupling services.

- **Azure Data Lake Storage**: Optimized for big data analytics.

Azure Blob Storage supports multiple tiers—Hot, Cool, and Archive—allowing for cost optimization based on access frequency.

Example of uploading a file to Blob Storage using Azure CLI:

```
az storage blob upload --account-name mystorageaccount --container-
name logs --file app.log --name app.log
```

Networking

Azure's networking stack allows you to create secure, performant, and globally distributed systems:

- **Azure Virtual Network (VNet)**: Private network for deploying resources.

- **Azure Application Gateway**: Layer 7 load balancing with Web Application Firewall (WAF).

- **Azure Front Door**: Global routing with SSL offloading and CDN capabilities.

- **ExpressRoute**: Dedicated private connection to Azure data centers.

Architects can combine these components to create multi-tiered applications with high availability and security.

Identity and Access Management

Identity is a foundational component of any secure system. Azure provides:

- **Azure Active Directory (Azure AD)**: Identity management for apps, users, and services.

- **Role-Based Access Control (RBAC)**: Granular permissions for Azure resources.

- **Managed Identities**: Automatic identity assignment for Azure services to access resources securely.

- **Conditional Access**: Policies that enforce MFA, geofencing, or device compliance.

Example of assigning a role to a user:

```
az role assignment create --assignee <userPrincipalName> --role
Contributor                                              --scope
/subscriptions/<subscriptionId>/resourceGroups/myResourceGroup
```

Databases and Analytics

Azure's data services range from traditional relational databases to modern real-time analytics platforms:

- **Azure SQL Database**: Managed relational database with auto-patching and backups.

- **Cosmos DB**: Globally distributed NoSQL database with multiple consistency models.

- **Azure Synapse Analytics**: Unified analytics platform for data warehousing and big data.

- **Azure Databricks**: Apache Spark-based analytics for AI/ML.

Azure also supports PostgreSQL, MySQL, and MongoDB, allowing flexibility in database choice.

Artificial Intelligence and Machine Learning

Azure is at the forefront of democratizing AI:

- **Azure Cognitive Services**: Prebuilt models for speech, vision, language, and decision-making.

- **Azure Machine Learning**: End-to-end platform for building, training, and deploying custom ML models.

- **OpenAI on Azure**: Enterprise-ready access to GPT models with compliance and data privacy.

Here's a Python example calling Azure's Text Analytics API:

```python
import requests

endpoint = "https://<your-region>.api.cognitive.microsoft.com/text/analytics/v3.0/sentiment"
headers = {"Ocp-Apim-Subscription-Key": "<your-key>", "Content-Type": "application/json"}
documents = {"documents": [{"id": "1", "language": "en", "text": "Azure is awesome!"}]}

response = requests.post(endpoint, headers=headers, json=documents)
print(response.json())
```

This allows developers to integrate AI into apps with minimal overhead.

Security, Governance, and Compliance

Azure is designed with security and compliance in mind. Native services include:

- **Microsoft Defender for Cloud**: Threat detection, security recommendations, and vulnerability assessments.

- **Azure Policy**: Enforce organizational standards and compliance rules.

- **Azure Blueprints**: Define repeatable environments with integrated policies and RBAC.

- **Key Vault**: Securely store and manage secrets, keys, and certificates.

Compliance is supported through extensive certification across industries and geographies, making Azure suitable for healthcare, finance, and government.

Hybrid and Multicloud Capabilities

Azure stands out for its hybrid capabilities, which are unmatched by most competitors:

- **Azure Arc**: Extend Azure services and governance to any infrastructure, including AWS and GCP.

- **Azure Stack**: Bring Azure services on-premises with hardware appliances.

- **Azure Lighthouse**: Manage multiple tenants from a single control plane.

These tools enable consistent management and governance across environments, reducing complexity and operational overhead.

Developer Ecosystem and Tooling

Microsoft's strong developer ecosystem is a major advantage:

- **Visual Studio and Visual Studio Code**: Deep Azure integrations, extensions, and debugging tools.

- **GitHub Actions**: CI/CD automation tightly integrated with Azure deployments.

- **Azure DevOps**: Project management, pipelines, repos, and test plans.

Sample pipeline YAML for an Azure Web App deployment:

```
trigger:
- main

pool:
  vmImage: 'ubuntu-latest'
```

```
steps:
- task: AzureWebApp@1
  inputs:
    azureSubscription: '<Your-Service-Connection>'
    appName: '<Your-App-Name>'
    package: '$(System.DefaultWorkingDirectory)/**/*.zip'
```

This helps automate deployments, enforce quality gates, and scale engineering workflows.

Community, Support, and Documentation

Azure benefits from:

- **Extensive Documentation**: Microsoft Learn, Quickstart templates, and tutorials.

- **Active Community**: Tech forums, GitHub repos, Stack Overflow, and Azure blogs.

- **Premier Support Plans**: Dedicated technical account managers and 24/7 support for mission-critical   applications.

Conclusion

Azure's platform capabilities span across compute, storage, networking, AI, DevOps, and security—all supported by a global infrastructure, compliance leadership, and tight integration with Microsoft's ecosystem. It is this holistic and enterprise-friendly approach that makes Azure a preferred choice for organizations architecting the future.

Whether you're building microservices, managing hybrid infrastructure, or deploying AI-driven apps, Azure offers the tools and ecosystem to bring your architecture to life. In the next section, we will explore the key principles that guide cloud architecture design and how they translate into real-world decisions.

Key Considerations in Cloud Design

Designing for the cloud is more than just lifting applications from on-premises environments and deploying them on virtual machines. It requires a shift in mindset that embraces distributed systems, automation, resilience, and continuous evolution. When using Microsoft Azure, architects must make a series of decisions that balance performance, cost, reliability, scalability, security, and maintainability. This section outlines the core considerations that shape modern cloud architecture on Azure.

Scalability and Elasticity

One of the cloud's biggest promises is elastic scalability—the ability to scale out (horizontal) or up (vertical) as needed. In Azure, this can be achieved in various ways:

- **Virtual Machine Scale Sets (VMSS)** allow identical VMs to scale automatically based on demand.

- **Azure App Service Plans** can scale web apps seamlessly without modifying code.

- **Azure Kubernetes Service (AKS)** supports scaling of containers using Horizontal Pod Autoscalers.

- **Azure Functions** are inherently elastic, scaling out based on event load.

When designing scalable systems, architects must consider:

- **Stateless Design**: Keeping services stateless allows them to scale easily without session stickiness.

- **Load Balancing**: Services like Azure Load Balancer and Application Gateway help distribute traffic across instances.

- **Concurrency Limits**: Understanding and tuning limits (e.g., max concurrent requests in Azure Functions).

A sample autoscale rule for an App Service might look like this (in ARM template syntax):

```
{
  "type": "Microsoft.Insights/autoscaleSettings",
  "name": "autoscaleSetting",
  "properties": {
    "targetResourceUri":              "[resourceId('Microsoft.Web/sites',
parameters('webAppName'))]",
    "enabled": true,
    "profiles": [
      {
        "name": "AutoScaleProfile",
        "capacity": {
          "minimum": "1",
          "maximum": "5",
          "default": "1"
        },
        "rules": [
          {
            "metricTrigger": {
```

```
        "metricName": "CpuPercentage",
        "operator": "GreaterThan",
        "threshold": 70,
        "timeGrain": "PT1M",
        "statistic": "Average",
        "timeWindow": "PT5M",
        "timeAggregation": "Average"
      },
      "scaleAction": {
        "direction": "Increase",
        "type": "ChangeCount",
        "value": "1",
        "cooldown": "PT1M"
      }
    }
  ]
  }
  ]
 }
}
```

This rule ensures your web app scales out as CPU usage increases.

Resilience and High Availability

Resilience is the system's ability to recover from failures and continue functioning. High availability (HA) ensures minimal downtime. In the cloud, failures are expected, so design patterns must anticipate and mitigate them.

Key strategies:

- **Availability Zones (AZs)**: Deploy resources across AZs to protect against data center failure.

- **Geo-replication**: Azure Storage and databases like Cosmos DB support replication across regions.

- **Retry Policies and Circuit Breakers**: Handle transient failures gracefully.

- **Backup and Restore**: Use Azure Backup, Azure Site Recovery, or database-specific features like geo-restore.

- **Traffic Manager**: Ensures users are directed to the healthiest endpoint globally.

Here's a simple example of using a retry policy in .NET:

```
HttpClient client = new HttpClient();
int retryCount = 3;

for (int i = 0; i < retryCount; i++)
{
    try
    {
        var              response              =              await
client.GetAsync("https://myapi.azurewebsites.net");
        if (response.IsSuccessStatusCode) break;
    }
    catch (HttpRequestException)
    {
        await Task.Delay(1000 * i); // Exponential backoff
    }
}
```

This basic loop retries the API call with increasing delay, improving resilience.

Cost Optimization

Cloud resources are metered, and every design choice has financial implications. Cost optimization involves not just reducing spend, but aligning cost with business value.

Considerations include:

- **Right-Sizing**: Choose the correct SKU and size based on workload. Use Azure Advisor for recommendations.

- **Reserved Instances (RIs)**: Prepay for one or three years to get significant discounts on VMs and databases.

- **Spot VMs**: Use for non-critical, interruptible workloads like batch processing.

- **Serverless Models**: Functions, Logic Apps, and Consumption Plans charge per execution, avoiding idle costs.

- **Shutdown Policies**: Automate shutdown of non-production environments during off-hours.

Example using Azure CLI to schedule shutdown for a VM:

```
az vm auto-shutdown --resource-group myResourceGroup --name myVM --
time 2200 --timezone "GMT Standard Time"
```

Additionally, use **Azure Cost Management + Billing** and **budgets/alerts** to track and control expenses proactively.

Security and Governance

Security must be foundational—not bolted on after deployment. Azure provides robust, native capabilities that span identity, access, data protection, and threat detection.

Best practices include:

- **Use Azure AD and MFA**: Centralized identity with enforced multi-factor authentication.

- **RBAC**: Assign users only the permissions they need.

- **Network Segmentation**: Use Network Security Groups (NSGs), Application Security Groups (ASGs), and firewalls.

- **Encryption**: Enable encryption at rest and in transit using customer-managed keys in Azure Key Vault.

- **Policy Enforcement**: Apply Azure Policy to block non-compliant deployments (e.g., open ports or untagged resources).

Example of assigning a policy to enforce location constraints:

```
az policy assignment create \
  --name "enforce-region" \
  --scope "/subscriptions/<sub-id>" \
  --policy
"/providers/Microsoft.Authorization/policyDefinitions/<policy-id>" \
  --params '{ "listOfAllowedLocations": { "value": ["UK South"] } }'
```

Security must be embedded throughout the software lifecycle. Consider DevSecOps tooling for code scanning, dependency checks, and pipeline enforcement.

Observability and Monitoring

Observability ensures that architects and operators can understand the internal state of a system from the outside. In Azure, observability is achieved through:

- **Azure Monitor**: Central hub for collecting metrics, logs, and telemetry.

- **Application Insights**: Tracks app performance, exceptions, and dependencies.

- **Log Analytics**: Query-based analysis using Kusto Query Language (KQL).

- **Alerts**: Notify teams based on thresholds, anomalies, or failure signals.

Sample KQL to find failed requests:

```
requests
| where success == false
| summarize count() by name, bin(timestamp, 1h)
```

This enables proactive diagnostics and root cause analysis. Integrate with **Azure Dashboards**, **Grafana**, or **Power BI** for visualization.

Automation and Infrastructure as Code

Manual deployments are error-prone and non-reproducible. Cloud architecture requires codification of everything from networks to policies using Infrastructure as Code (IaC).

Azure supports multiple IaC tools:

- **ARM Templates**: JSON-based declarative definitions.

- **Bicep**: Simpler, modular syntax for ARM templates.

- **Terraform**: Popular third-party tool for cloud-agnostic deployments.

- **Azure DevOps/GitHub Actions**: Automate build, test, and deployment pipelines.

Example of Bicep to deploy a storage account:

```
resource storage 'Microsoft.Storage/storageAccounts@2022-09-01' = {
  name: 'mystorageacct'
  location: 'eastus'
  sku: {
    name: 'Standard_LRS'
  }
  kind: 'StorageV2'
  properties: {
    accessTier: 'Hot'
  }
}
```

IaC promotes consistency, version control, and repeatable deployments. Use CI/CD pipelines to automate from commit to deployment.

Modularity and Reusability

Cloud systems should be designed in modular components that can be reused and iterated upon independently. This principle applies across:

- **Infrastructure**: Modular Bicep or Terraform modules.

- **Applications**: Microservices and APIs.

- **Security**: Policy packs and reusable role definitions.

- **Monitoring**: Centralized dashboards and alert templates.

For instance, in Terraform, creating a reusable module for networking:

```
module "network" {
  source = "./modules/network"
  vnet_name = "my-vnet"
  address_space = ["10.0.0.0/16"]
}
```

Modularity ensures faster onboarding, reduces duplication, and simplifies testing.

Performance Optimization

Architects must consider not only whether systems scale, but how efficiently they perform under load. This includes:

- **Caching**: Use Azure Cache for Redis to reduce latency and offload backends.

- **Data Partitioning**: For large-scale databases, partition data across storage accounts or databases.

- **CDNs**: Use Azure CDN or Azure Front Door to cache static content near the user.

- **Query Tuning**: Use Query Store in Azure SQL or diagnostics in Cosmos DB to analyze and optimize.

Example of configuring Azure Front Door for global caching:

```
az network front-door create \
  --resource-group myResourceGroup \
```

```
--name myFrontDoor \
--backend-address www.mybackend.com \
--accepted-protocols Http Https
```

Use load testing tools like **Azure Load Testing** to simulate traffic and benchmark responsiveness.

Compliance and Data Residency

Many industries are subject to strict data handling regulations. Azure helps meet these through:

- **Region Selection**: Choose where data is stored and processed.

- **Data Classification**: Label and encrypt sensitive information.

- **Retention Policies**: Define how long data is stored and when it is purged.

- **Audit Trails**: Use Azure Monitor and Microsoft Purview for activity logging.

Example of setting data retention in Log Analytics:

```
az monitor log-analytics workspace update \
  --resource-group myResourceGroup \
  --workspace-name myWorkspace \
  --retention-time 365
```

Ensure that designs accommodate jurisdictional and sector-specific regulations from the start.

Conclusion

Cloud design is an exercise in trade-offs. A successful Azure architecture balances performance, cost, security, and flexibility through careful planning and adherence to architectural best practices. It uses the full spectrum of Azure services—not just as tools, but as enablers of automation, resilience, and innovation.

As the foundation of your journey into Azure architecture, these considerations will inform every deployment, service selection, and governance model you adopt. In the next chapter, we will dive into Azure's core services, exploring how they can be combined to create powerful, scalable, and secure solutions.

Chapter 2: Core Azure Services for Architects

Azure Compute Options: VMs, App Services, and Containers

In any cloud architecture, compute is a fundamental layer that determines how applications and services are executed. Azure provides a flexible and robust suite of compute options designed to meet a wide range of workloads—from traditional virtual machines to modern containerized and serverless applications. Understanding when and how to use these services is critical for designing performant, cost-efficient, and maintainable systems.

This section explores the three most widely used Azure compute options: **Virtual Machines (VMs)**, **App Services**, and **Containers**. Each has distinct strengths, use cases, and operational considerations. Choosing the right compute model often depends on factors such as workload type, scalability requirements, deployment frequency, and the level of control needed over the underlying infrastructure.

Azure Virtual Machines

Azure Virtual Machines offer Infrastructure-as-a-Service (IaaS), giving architects the most control over the operating system, runtime, and application stack. This makes them suitable for legacy applications, custom runtimes, and software that hasn't been adapted to run in PaaS or container environments.

Key Features

- Support for Windows and Linux OS

- Extensive VM sizes for general, memory-, and compute-optimized workloads

- Availability Sets and Zones for high availability

- Custom images and shared image galleries

- Integration with Azure Backup, Azure Site Recovery, and Azure Monitor

Use Cases

- Running traditional or legacy enterprise applications

- Hosting databases like SQL Server or Oracle (outside managed offerings)

- Custom software that requires specific OS or kernel-level modifications

- Applications that must persist local state

Example: Provisioning a VM using Azure CLI

```
az vm create \
  --resource-group myResourceGroup \
  --name myVM \
  --image UbuntuLTS \
  --admin-username azureuser \
  --generate-ssh-keys
```

Best Practices

- Always use managed disks for reliability.

- Enable automatic updates and security baselines.

- Use Azure Bastion for secure VM access without exposing SSH/RDP ports.

- Use tagging and Azure Policy to manage and govern VM resources.

VMs offer the most control but require substantial operational effort for updates, security, and availability.

Azure App Services

App Services are part of Azure's Platform-as-a-Service (PaaS) offerings and abstract away infrastructure concerns so developers can focus purely on application logic. App Services support .NET, Node.js, Python, Java, PHP, and custom Docker containers.

Key Features

- Auto-scaling and load balancing built-in

- Integrated CI/CD with GitHub or Azure DevOps

- Deployment slots for zero-downtime deployments

- Custom domains and SSL bindings

- Staging and production environments

Use Cases

- Web apps and RESTful APIs
- Lightweight backend services for mobile or IoT
- Business logic layers in multi-tier apps
- Single-page applications hosted with backend APIs

Example: Deploying an App Service with Azure CLI

```
az appservice plan create --name myAppServicePlan --resource-group
myResourceGroup --sku B1 --is-linux
az webapp create --resource-group myResourceGroup --plan
myAppServicePlan --name myUniqueApp --runtime "NODE|18-lts"
```

You can push your app to this web service via `az webapp deployment source config`.

Best Practices

- Use deployment slots for blue/green and canary releases.
- Integrate with Azure Monitor and Application Insights for telemetry.
- Use Managed Identity to access other Azure resources securely.
- Leverage scaling rules based on metrics (e.g., CPU, memory, queue length).

App Services simplify lifecycle management and are ideal for developers looking to deploy quickly and iterate often.

Azure Containers and Azure Kubernetes Service

Containers provide lightweight, portable environments for applications and their dependencies. They are ideal for microservices, scalable APIs, and stateless workloads. Azure offers several ways to deploy containers:

- **Azure Container Instances (ACI)**: Run a container with no orchestration.
- **Azure Kubernetes Service (AKS)**: Fully managed Kubernetes cluster for complex containerized applications.
- **App Service for Containers**: Deploy custom containers in PaaS.

Azure Container Instances (ACI)

ACI is a simple option for running containers without managing VMs or orchestrators.

```
az container create \
  --resource-group myResourceGroup \
  --name myContainer \
  --image mcr.microsoft.com/azuredocs/aci-helloworld \
  --dns-name-label aci-demo \
  --ports 80
```

Use cases include batch jobs, cron tasks, and test environments.

Azure Kubernetes Service (AKS)

AKS enables production-grade Kubernetes deployments with features like scaling, monitoring, and RBAC baked in.

Key Features

- Integrated with Azure AD, Monitor, and Policy
- Supports Helm, KEDA, and Azure Dev Spaces
- Node pools for different workloads
- Built-in ingress controllers and service meshes

Example: Creating an AKS Cluster

```
az aks create \
  --resource-group myResourceGroup \
  --name myAKSCluster \
  --node-count 3 \
  --enable-addons monitoring \
  --generate-ssh-keys
```

You can then interact with the cluster using kubectl:

```
az aks get-credentials --resource-group myResourceGroup --name myAKSCluster
kubectl get nodes
```

Best Practices

- Use separate namespaces for environments (dev, staging, prod).

- Enable auto-scaling and define resource limits for pods.

- Use Azure Container Registry (ACR) for private images.

- Automate deployments using GitOps or CI/CD pipelines.

AKS is powerful but introduces operational complexity. It is best suited for large-scale, container-first applications with mature DevOps pipelines.

Choosing the Right Compute Model

Criteria	Virtual Machines	App Services	Containers (ACI/AKS)
Control	Full	Medium	High (AKS), Low (ACI)
Ease of Deployment	Medium	High	Medium
Scalability	Manual/Scripted	Auto-scaling	Auto-scaling
Cost Optimization	Reserved/Spot VMs	Consumption Plans	Pay-per-second (ACI)
Best For	Legacy apps, DBs	Web apps, APIs	Microservices, batch jobs

The selection is often not binary. Many solutions use a **polyglot compute** strategy—for example, combining App Services for APIs, Functions for events, and AKS for backend services.

Integration with Other Azure Services

Regardless of compute type, integration with other Azure services is essential:

- **Azure Monitor** for centralized logging and metrics

- **Key Vault** for secrets and certificates

- **Application Gateway** or **Front Door** for traffic routing

- **Storage Accounts** or **Cosmos DB** for persistent data

Designing compute in isolation leads to bottlenecks and blind spots. It's important to architect the compute layer as a seamless part of a larger system.

Deployment Pipelines and CI/CD

Deployment strategies differ based on the compute choice:

- **App Services** can deploy directly via GitHub Actions or Azure DevOps.

- **VMs** require scripting (e.g., PowerShell, DSC, Ansible).

- **Containers** integrate with Docker registries and Helm charts.

- **AKS** often leverages GitOps (e.g., Flux, Argo CD) or YAML-based pipelines.

Sample GitHub Action for App Service:

```
name: Deploy to Azure Web App
on:
  push:
    branches:
      - main
jobs:
  build-and-deploy:
    runs-on: ubuntu-latest
    steps:
      - uses: actions/checkout@v2
      - uses: azure/webapps-deploy@v2
        with:
          app-name: myUniqueApp
          publish-profile: ${{ secrets.AZURE_WEBAPP_PUBLISH_PROFILE
}}
          package: .
```

This pipeline ensures that every push to main results in an automatic deployment.

Conclusion

Azure's compute options are powerful, diverse, and designed for flexibility. Whether you need full control over a machine, want to deploy a web app without managing infrastructure, or scale containerized workloads across a cluster, Azure provides a well-integrated ecosystem to meet your needs.

The decision between VMs, App Services, and Containers should be driven by application requirements, operational maturity, and business goals. Often, a hybrid approach yields the most value—leveraging the strengths of each model across different layers of the application.

In the next section, we will dive deeper into Azure Storage services—another foundational pillar of cloud architecture—exploring how they support structured, unstructured, and high-throughput data workloads.

Azure Storage Fundamentals

Storage is the backbone of nearly every cloud-native architecture. Whether you're building a web application, processing big data, or managing IoT streams, storage plays a vital role in data persistence, accessibility, scalability, and security. Azure offers a wide range of storage services that cater to different types of data—structured, semi-structured, unstructured—and usage patterns. Understanding Azure Storage fundamentals is essential for architects seeking to design efficient, scalable, and secure cloud systems.

This section explores the major types of Azure Storage services, their key features, access methods, performance tiers, and practical considerations for architects.

Core Storage Services in Azure

Azure provides a unified storage account abstraction that can serve multiple types of data services:

1. **Azure Blob Storage** – Optimized for storing massive amounts of unstructured data like images, video, documents, and backups.

2. **Azure File Storage** – Provides shared access to files using the SMB protocol, suitable for lift-and-shift of legacy applications.

3. **Azure Queue Storage** – Offers message queuing for communication between distributed services.

4. **Azure Table Storage** – A NoSQL key-value store for structured data.

5. **Azure Disk Storage** – Managed virtual hard disks for VMs.

Each of these services is accessible via a common **Azure Storage Account**, which can be of two major types:

- **General-purpose v2 (GPv2)** – Supports all features, tiers, and storage types.

- **Blob Storage account** – Specialized for unstructured object data (useful for large-scale blob-only use cases).

Azure Blob Storage

Blob Storage is one of the most popular and versatile storage services in Azure. It supports three types of blobs:

- **Block blobs** – Used for storing text and binary files, optimized for upload performance.

- **Append blobs** – Ideal for logging scenarios where data is appended sequentially.

- **Page blobs** – Designed for random read/write operations, mainly used for VHDs and disks.

Tiers of Blob Storage

Azure Blob Storage supports multiple access tiers, allowing you to optimize cost based on data access patterns:

- **Hot Tier** – Optimized for frequent access. Higher storage cost, lower access cost.

- **Cool Tier** – For infrequently accessed data. Lower storage cost, higher access cost.

- **Archive Tier** – For rarely accessed, long-term storage. Extremely low storage cost, but high latency for retrieval.

You can set the tier when uploading data or move it via lifecycle rules.

```
az storage blob upload \
  --account-name mystorageaccount \
  --container-name logs \
  --name app.log \
  --file ./app.log \
  --tier Cool
```

Security and Access

- **SAS Tokens**: Generate short-lived tokens for secure, time-bound access.

- **Managed Identities**: Use Azure AD to securely access storage without secrets.

- **Encryption**: Data is encrypted at rest using Microsoft-managed or customer-managed keys.

Use Cases

- Backup and archival
- Streaming media
- Data lakes (especially when combined with Azure Data Lake Storage Gen2)
- Web content hosting (static websites)

Azure File Storage

Azure Files offers fully managed file shares in the cloud accessible via the SMB or NFS protocols. Unlike traditional file servers, Azure File Shares are scalable and highly available by default.

Key Features

- SMB 3.0 support for on-premises mounting
- Snapshot support for point-in-time recovery
- Azure File Sync for hybrid deployments
- Supports private endpoints and Active Directory authentication

```
az storage share-rm create \
  --resource-group myResourceGroup \
  --storage-account mystorageaccount \
  --name myshare \
  --quota 100
```

Once the share is created, you can mount it on Windows or Linux using the connection string provided by Azure.

Use Cases

- Migrating legacy file servers to the cloud
- Shared application configuration
- Hosting lift-and-shift applications that require file system access
- Hybrid workloads with Azure File Sync

Azure Queue Storage

Queue Storage enables decoupled communication between application components, following the **producer-consumer** pattern. It is part of Azure's messaging stack, which also includes Service Bus and Event Grid.

Key Features

- FIFO (First In, First Out) message queuing

- Message TTL and dequeue visibility timeouts

- Peek, dequeue, delete, and update operations

```
az storage queue create \
  --name taskqueue \
  --account-name mystorageaccount
```

Developers can send and process messages via SDKs or REST APIs. This pattern enhances scalability and fault tolerance.

Use Cases

- Workload decoupling

- Background job scheduling

- Asynchronous task processing

Azure Table Storage

Table Storage is a NoSQL key-value store that offers fast access to large datasets with a flexible schema.

Features

- Scalable to billions of rows

- Partition key and row key indexing for fast retrieval

- Pay-per-use model

```
az storage table create \
  --name UserProfileTable \
  --account-name mystorageaccount
```

Although Table Storage is still available, many modern applications are moving to **Azure Cosmos DB**, which offers similar APIs but with global distribution, richer query support, and stronger consistency models.

Use Cases

- Audit   logs

- User   profiles

- Lightweight   telemetry   data

- IoT   metadata

Azure Disk Storage

Disk Storage provides persistent disks for Azure Virtual Machines. These are available in different performance tiers:

- **Standard HDD** – Cost-effective for infrequent access.

- **Standard SSD** – Low latency for web servers and entry-level workloads.

- **Premium SSD** – High IOPS for databases and latency-sensitive workloads.

- **Ultra Disk** – Extreme performance for data-intensive apps.

Azure Disk encryption ensures data is encrypted at rest. Snapshots allow for backup and restore workflows.

Example: Attach a new disk to an existing VM

```
az vm disk attach \
  --vm-name myVM \
  --disk myDataDisk \
  --resource-group myResourceGroup
```

Use Cases

- Persistent   storage   for   VMs

- Database   file   storage   (e.g.,   SQL   Server   MDF,   LDF   files)

- High-throughput   batch   processing

Storage Access Options

Azure supports multiple ways to access storage:

- **REST APIs** for programmatic control
- **SDKs** in .NET, Java, Python, Node.js
- **Azure Storage Explorer** GUI tool
- **azcopy** for command-line transfers
- **Mounting shares** directly in OS

Example using `azcopy`:

```
azcopy copy
'https://mystorageaccount.blob.core.windows.net/mycontainer/myfile.t
xt' './myfile.txt'
```

Networking and Security

To restrict access to storage resources:

- Use **private endpoints** to map storage to a VNet.
- Implement **service endpoints** to limit access to trusted subnets.
- Enforce **firewall rules** at the storage account level.
- Configure **shared access policies** for granular control.

For compliance, ensure that diagnostic logs are enabled and retention policies are configured to meet regulatory requirements.

Monitoring and Optimization

To maintain performance and cost-efficiency:

- Use **Azure Monitor** to track storage metrics (e.g., availability, latency, egress).
- Set **lifecycle management rules** to move blobs to cooler tiers or delete expired data.
- Review **Azure Advisor** recommendations for cost and performance improvements.

Example of a basic lifecycle rule in JSON:

```json
{
  "rules": [
    {
      "enabled": true,
      "name": "archive-old-blobs",
      "type": "Lifecycle",
      "definition": {
        "filters": {
          "blobTypes": ["blockBlob"],
          "prefixMatch": ["logs/"]
        },
        "actions": {
          "baseBlob": {
            "tierToArchive": { "daysAfterModificationGreaterThan": 30
}
          }
        }
      }
    }
  ]
}
```

You can apply these rules using Azure CLI or through the portal.

Design Considerations for Architects

When designing systems that rely on Azure Storage:

- **Durability**: Data is replicated within and across regions using options like LRS, GRS, ZRS.

- **Latency**: Choose regions close to users or edge locations.

- **Scalability**: Architect for parallel uploads/downloads and use batch operations.

- **Security**: Adopt a least-privilege approach with RBAC and SAS tokens.

- **Compliance**: Understand and implement required data retention and encryption standards.

Conclusion

Azure Storage is a powerful, scalable, and secure foundation for modern applications. It offers a wide range of storage options, each tailored to specific scenarios—whether you're archiving log data, serving web content, processing asynchronous workloads, or hosting enterprise file shares. Properly leveraging Azure's storage services enables cloud architects to design systems that are cost-effective, performant, and resilient.

In the next section, we will explore Azure's networking services and how they enable secure, performant, and scalable communication between resources, applications, and end users.

Networking with Azure Virtual Network (VNet)

Networking is the glue that connects cloud resources to one another and to the outside world. In Microsoft Azure, the **Virtual Network (VNet)** is the foundational building block for networking within the platform. It provides secure, private communication between Azure services, on-premises infrastructure, and external networks, all while enabling control over IP address spaces, subnets, routing, and security.

Azure Virtual Network is a highly configurable and scalable component of any architecture and plays a central role in achieving goals related to **performance, security, availability, and compliance**. This section provides a deep dive into VNets, exploring design patterns, integration options, security controls, and best practices for architects.

What is Azure Virtual Network?

Azure Virtual Network is an IaaS service that enables users to provision private IP address spaces, connect virtual machines and services, and define their communication rules. Think of it as your cloud-based version of an on-premises data center network.

Key properties:

- **Private IP addressing using RFC1918** ranges (10.x, 172.16.x, 192.168.x)

- **Custom subnets** with CIDR notation

- **Route tables**, **DNS settings**, and **Network Security Groups**

- **Peering**, **VPNs**, and **ExpressRoute** for external connectivity

A basic VNet structure might include subnets for different roles—frontend, backend, database—and connectivity to a hub network for shared services.

Creating a Virtual Network

A VNet can be created via the Azure Portal, CLI, ARM, or Terraform.

Azure CLI Example

```
az network vnet create \
```

```
--resource-group myResourceGroup \
--name myVNet \
--address-prefix 10.0.0.0/16 \
--subnet-name mySubnet \
--subnet-prefix 10.0.1.0/24
```

This command provisions a new virtual network with a single subnet. Additional subnets can be added later to segregate workloads.

Subnets and IP Address Planning

When designing a VNet, it's crucial to plan the IP address ranges in advance. Overlapping CIDR blocks can lead to peering issues. Subnets should be allocated based on roles and isolated for performance and security.

Typical subnet strategy:

- **10.0.1.0/24** – Web Tier
- **10.0.2.0/24** – App Tier
- **10.0.3.0/24** – Database Tier
- **10.0.4.0/24** – Gateway Subnet (required for VPN/ExpressRoute)

Larger networks may include separate **hub** and **spoke** networks, with centralized routing and monitoring in the hub.

Peering Virtual Networks

VNet Peering allows seamless connectivity between two VNets—either in the same region or across regions—using Azure's backbone.

Key Properties

- Low latency and high bandwidth
- Private IP communication across VNets
- Option to allow or disallow transit routing

Peering Example (CLI)

```
az network vnet peering create \
  --name LinkVNet1ToVNet2 \
  --resource-group myResourceGroup \
```

```
 --vnet-name VNet1 \
 --remote-vnet                          /subscriptions/<sub-
id>/resourceGroups/otherGroup/providers/Microsoft.Network/virtualNet
works/VNet2 \
 --allow-vnet-access
```

Use cases:

- **Hub-and-Spoke Architecture**: Centralized control and services in the hub (e.g., firewalls, DNS).

- **Multi-Region Deployments**: Disaster recovery, geo-distribution, or data residency.

- **Team Isolation**: Isolate workloads in separate VNets but allow controlled communication.

Route Tables and UDRs

Azure automatically creates system routes for VNets, but architects can override these with **User-Defined Routes (UDRs)**. This is useful for directing traffic through **Network Virtual Appliances (NVAs)** or **firewalls**.

Example: Forcing traffic to go through a virtual appliance.

```
az network route-table create --name MyRouteTable --resource-group
myResourceGroup
az network route-table route create \
  --resource-group myResourceGroup \
  --route-table-name MyRouteTable \
  --name ToFirewall \
  --address-prefix 0.0.0.0/0 \
  --next-hop-type VirtualAppliance \
  --next-hop-ip-address 10.0.4.4
az network vnet subnet update \
  --vnet-name myVNet \
  --name mySubnet \
  --route-table MyRouteTable
```

Use route tables to define:

- Internet   breakouts

- Forced tunneling to on-prem firewalls

- Inter-subnet routing restrictions

Network Security Groups (NSGs)

NSGs are essential for securing traffic within VNets. They act as stateful firewalls, controlling both inbound and outbound traffic at the subnet or NIC level.

Each rule in an NSG has:

- **Priority**: 100–4096 (lower number = higher priority)

- **Direction**: Inbound or Outbound

- **Protocol**: TCP, UDP, or *

- **Source/Destination**: IP ranges or tags (e.g., Internet, VirtualNetwork)

- **Port Range**: e.g., 80, 443

- **Action**: Allow or Deny

Example rule to allow HTTP traffic:

```
az network nsg rule create \
  --resource-group myResourceGroup \
  --nsg-name myNSG \
  --name AllowHTTP \
  --priority 100 \
  --direction Inbound \
  --access Allow \
  --protocol Tcp \
  --destination-port-range 80 \
  --source-address-prefix Internet \
  --destination-address-prefix '*'
```

Use NSGs to enforce zero trust principles, isolate workloads, and limit exposure.

DNS and Name Resolution

Azure provides internal DNS for name resolution of resources within a VNet. However, you can also configure custom DNS servers for:

- Private name resolution (e.g., internal domain names)

- Integration with on-prem Active Directory

- Forwarding to public DNS as needed

Set DNS servers at the VNet level:

```
az network vnet update \
  --name myVNet \
  --resource-group myResourceGroup \
  --dns-servers 10.0.5.4 10.0.5.5
```

Consider using **Azure Private DNS Zones** to manage internal names in hybrid and microservice environments.

Hybrid Connectivity

Many architectures require secure communication between Azure and on-premises environments. Azure supports several methods:

VPN Gateway

- **Site-to-Site VPN**: IPSec-based tunnel between on-prem and Azure.

- **Point-to-Site VPN**: Users connect securely from remote locations.

- **VNet-to-VNet VPN**: Secure communication between VNets.

Provisioning a VPN Gateway:

```
az network vnet-gateway create \
  --resource-group myResourceGroup \
  --name myVpnGateway \
  --public-ip-address myPublicIP \
  --vnet myVNet \
  --gateway-type Vpn \
  --sku VpnGw1 \
  --vpn-type RouteBased
```

ExpressRoute

For high-throughput, low-latency, private connections to Azure from on-prem:

- SLA-backed connectivity

- Private peering with Microsoft services

- Ideal for sensitive, regulated workloads

ExpressRoute requires coordination with a connectivity provider.

Private Endpoints and Service Endpoints

To secure PaaS services within a VNet:

- **Service Endpoints**: Extend VNet identity to services like Azure Storage or SQL, keeping traffic on the Azure backbone.

- **Private Endpoints**: Map services to private IPs within a subnet, entirely removing public exposure.

Example of creating a private endpoint for an Azure Storage account:

```
az network private-endpoint create \
  --name myPrivateEndpoint \
  --resource-group myResourceGroup \
  --vnet-name myVNet \
  --subnet mySubnet \
  --private-connection-resource-id           /subscriptions/<sub-
id>/resourceGroups/myRG/providers/Microsoft.Storage/storageAccounts/
myStorage \
  --group-id blob
```

Private endpoints are ideal for high-security environments where public access must be avoided entirely.

Monitoring and Diagnostics

Use the following tools to monitor and troubleshoot networking:

- **Network Watcher**: Packet capture, topology diagrams, IP flow verify.

- **Connection Monitor**: Continuous monitoring of connectivity and performance.

- **NSG Flow Logs**: Detailed traffic logs for auditing and analytics.

- **Metrics and Alerts**: Trigger alerts based on bandwidth, connection failures, etc.

Enable flow logs:

```
az network watcher flow-log configure \
  --resource-group myResourceGroup \
  --nsg myNSG \
  --enabled true \
  --storage-account myStorage \
  --retention 7
```

Export diagnostic data to Log Analytics for deep insights using Kusto Query Language (KQL).

High Availability and Redundancy

For mission-critical workloads, networking design must avoid single points of failure:

- Use **Availability Zones** for zonal redundancy of gateways and load balancers.

- Deploy **Active/Active** **VPN** **gateways**.

- Route traffic through **Azure Load Balancer** (Layer 4) or **Application Gateway** (Layer 7).

- Use **Azure Front Door** for global traffic distribution with health probes.

Example of configuring a Basic Load Balancer:

```
az network lb create \
  --name myLoadBalancer \
  --resource-group myResourceGroup \
  --sku Basic \
  --frontend-ip-name myFrontEnd \
  --backend-pool-name myBackEndPool \
  --vnet-name myVNet
```

Always design for failover, both within and across regions.

Best Practices and Design Patterns

- **Segment traffic** using subnets and NSGs for tiered architectures (web, app, data).

- **Use hub-and-spoke topology** for multi-VNet solutions, centralizing common services.

- **Apply least privilege** for all NSGs and route tables.

- **Enable DDoS Protection Standard** for critical workloads.

- **Plan IP ranges** to avoid overlap for future peering or hybrid expansion.

- **Document and version** network designs using Infrastructure as Code (Bicep, Terraform).

Conclusion

Azure Virtual Network is a powerful and flexible foundation for secure and performant communication in the cloud. Whether you're deploying isolated microservices or building hybrid enterprise solutions, a well-designed network architecture ensures scalability, control, and resilience.

In the next section, we will explore the tools and services Azure provides for monitoring and managing cloud environments, ensuring that your infrastructure remains healthy, compliant, and cost-efficient.

Monitoring and Management Tools

Effective monitoring and management are essential pillars of any reliable, scalable, and secure cloud architecture. Without visibility into system behavior, performance bottlenecks, availability issues, or security incidents can go undetected until they cause significant disruption. In Azure, monitoring is not an afterthought—it's a fully integrated part of the platform, offering deep insights and automation capabilities across infrastructure, applications, and services.

Azure provides a suite of monitoring and management tools that help you track resource health, diagnose issues, implement governance, and continuously optimize operations. This section explores these tools in detail, including **Azure Monitor**, **Log Analytics**, **Application Insights**, **Azure Advisor**, **Azure Automation**, and **Azure Resource Graph**—with practical examples and architectural best practices.

Azure Monitor: The Central Monitoring Hub

Azure Monitor is the umbrella service for all monitoring data in Azure. It collects and stores metrics, logs, and traces from nearly every Azure resource and provides visualization, alerting, and automation.

Core Capabilities

- **Metrics**: Numeric data collected at regular intervals (e.g., CPU usage, disk IOPS).

- **Logs**: Structured and unstructured data such as events, activity logs, diagnostics, and performance   counters.

- **Alerts**:   Trigger   actions   based   on   thresholds   or   conditions.

- **Dashboards**:   Visualize   telemetry   with   customizable   dashboards.

- **Workbooks**:   Predefined   templates   for   rich,   interactive   reports.

Enabling Monitoring on Resources

By default, many Azure services emit metrics. For logs, you often need to enable diagnostic settings.

```
az monitor diagnostic-settings create \
  --resource                                    /subscriptions/<sub-
id>/resourceGroups/myResourceGroup/providers/Microsoft.Compute/virtu
alMachines/myVM \
  --name "vmDiagnostics" \
  --workspace <log-analytics-workspace-id> \
  --metrics '[{"category":"AllMetrics","enabled":true}]' \
  --logs '[{"category":"AuditLogs","enabled":true}]'
```

Diagnostic settings route logs to Log Analytics, Event Hubs, or Storage for long-term analysis.

Log Analytics and Kusto Query Language (KQL)

Log Analytics is the data platform for querying logs collected by Azure Monitor. It uses **Kusto Query Language (KQL)**, a powerful syntax for analyzing time-series and event data.

Sample KQL Queries

Identify failed VM logins:

```
SecurityEvent
| where EventID == 4625
| summarize count() by Account
```

Find top IPs making requests to a web app:

```
AppRequests
| summarize count() by client_IP
```

```
| top 10 by count_
```

KQL supports joins, aggregation, filters, and machine learning models, making it suitable for deep operational and security insights.

Application Insights

Application Insights is tailored for developers and application monitoring. It collects telemetry data from your app, including:

- Request rates, durations, failures

- Exception tracking

- Dependency performance (SQL, HTTP calls)

- Custom events and metrics

- Live metrics and user session tracking

Supported platforms include .NET, Java, Node.js, Python, and more.

Example: Integrate Application Insights in ASP.NET Core

```
public void ConfigureServices(IServiceCollection services)
{

services.AddApplicationInsightsTelemetry(Configuration["ApplicationI
nsights:InstrumentationKey"]);
}
```

Once integrated, you can view request timelines, diagnose exceptions, track release health, and identify performance regressions.

Use Application Map to visualize service dependencies and investigate latency sources.

Azure Advisor

Azure Advisor provides actionable recommendations to improve reliability, performance, security, and cost-effectiveness of your workloads. It analyzes your deployed resources and flags:

- Underutilized VMs

- Security vulnerabilities

- Unused IPs or NICs

- Availability zone suggestions

- Cost optimization opportunities

```
az advisor recommendation list --output table
```

Each recommendation includes estimated impact, justification, and remediation steps. Use Advisor as part of regular health reviews and FinOps strategy.

Alerts and Action Groups

Alerts enable proactive response to system changes or performance issues. Azure supports:

- **Metric alerts**: Triggered by numeric thresholds (e.g., CPU > 80% for 5 mins).

- **Log alerts**: Based on KQL query results.

- **Activity log alerts**: For management operations (e.g., resource deletion).

Action Groups define what happens when an alert fires—such as sending an email, calling a webhook, or triggering an Azure Function.

Example: CPU Threshold Alert

```
az monitor metrics alert create \
  --name "HighCPUAlert" \
  --resource-group myResourceGroup \
  --scopes                              "/subscriptions/<sub-
id>/resourceGroups/myResourceGroup/providers/Microsoft.Compute/virtu
alMachines/myVM" \
  --condition "avg Percentage CPU > 80" \
  --description "Alert when CPU > 80%" \
  --action-group myActionGroup
```

Alerts are essential for production readiness, SLAs, and continuous operations.

Azure Automation

Azure Automation provides a platform to create, schedule, and manage runbooks for operational tasks like patching, scaling, or compliance enforcement.

Use cases:

- Auto-shutdown/start VMs based on business hours
- Cleanup of unused resources
- Configuration management via Desired State Configuration (DSC)

Example: PowerShell Runbook to Stop a VM

```
param(
    [string]$ResourceGroupName,
    [string]$VMName
)
Stop-AzVM -ResourceGroupName $ResourceGroupName -Name $VMName -Force
```

Runbooks can be scheduled or triggered via webhooks and integrated with alerts for automated remediation.

Azure Resource Graph

Resource Graph enables exploration and inventory management across your Azure environment using a high-performance query engine.

It helps answer questions like:

- What resources are untagged?
- Which VMs are in a specific region?
- Which resources are not compliant with policy?

Example: Find All VMs Without Tags

```
Resources
| where type =~ 'microsoft.compute/virtualmachines'
| where tags == ''
| project name, location, resourceGroup
```

Resource Graph Explorer is ideal for governance, security audits, and large-scale discovery across subscriptions.

Azure Service Health and Resource Health

These services help differentiate between platform-wide issues and resource-specific problems.

- **Service Health**: Notifies you of Azure-wide outages, maintenance, and incidents.

- **Resource Health**: Shows the availability state of individual resources over time (e.g., VM unresponsive due to hardware).

Integrate Service Health alerts into action groups for enterprise incident response.

Azure Cost Management

Monitoring isn't limited to performance—it includes cost.

Azure Cost Management + Billing allows you to:

- Track usage by service, resource group, or tag

- Set budgets with email alerts

- Forecast future spend

- Export data for analysis

Create a budget with alerts:

```
az consumption budget create \
  --amount 100 \
  --time-grain monthly \
  --name MonthlyBudget \
  --resource-group myResourceGroup \
  --category cost \
  --notification key1 \
  --operator GreaterThan \
  --threshold 80 \
  --contact-emails admin@example.com
```

Incorporate cost monitoring into your architecture reviews to avoid sprawl and optimize ROI.

Azure Monitor Workbooks

Workbooks provide a dynamic, interactive canvas for combining visualizations, text, and analytics. Use workbooks to create:

- Compliance dashboards

- Application health overviews

- SRE and NOC operation dashboards

Built-in templates make it easy to get started, and workbooks can be shared and customized to meet specific stakeholder needs.

Integrations with External Tools

Azure's monitoring services integrate well with third-party tools like:

- **Grafana**: Native Azure Monitor plugin for real-time dashboards

- **Datadog**: Full-stack observability across Azure and hybrid

- **Splunk, Elastic**: Ingest log data via Event Hub

Use webhooks, Logic Apps, or Event Grid to connect alert events to external systems like Slack, ServiceNow, or PagerDuty.

Management at Scale with Azure Policy

While Azure Monitor focuses on observability, **Azure Policy** supports governance and management at scale.

Examples:

- Enforce tagging rules

- Restrict resource locations

- Audit unencrypted storage accounts

- Block public IP assignments

Apply policies programmatically:

```
az policy assignment create \
  --name enforce-tagging \
  --policy
/providers/Microsoft.Authorization/policyDefinitions/require-tag \
  --params '{ "tagName": { "value": "Environment" } }' \
  --scope /subscriptions/<sub-id>
```

Pair policies with monitoring to create a secure and compliant environment by design.

Conclusion

Monitoring and management are not just support functions—they are central to the success of cloud architectures. With Azure's rich ecosystem of tools like Monitor, Application Insights, Log Analytics, and Automation, architects can build systems that are **resilient, observable, secure, and efficient**.

By establishing a strong monitoring baseline, integrating alerts and automation, and continuously optimizing based on data-driven insights, organizations can not only meet but exceed SLAs, ensure compliance, and deliver exceptional user experiences.

In the next chapter, we'll turn our attention to performance and scalability—exploring how to design architectures that dynamically adapt to user load, application complexity, and evolving business needs.

Chapter 3: Designing for Performance and Scalability

Autoscaling Strategies in Azure

Autoscaling is a fundamental principle in cloud architecture that enables applications to dynamically adjust resource allocation based on workload demand. In the traditional on-premises model, infrastructure had to be provisioned for peak capacity, often leading to underutilization. Azure's autoscaling capabilities allow cloud-native systems to scale efficiently, improving both performance and cost-effectiveness.

Autoscaling ensures optimal resource usage, high availability, and consistent performance under varying loads. Azure provides autoscaling at multiple levels—from virtual machines to platform-as-a-service (PaaS) offerings and containers. This section explores the autoscaling mechanisms available in Azure, how they function, when to use them, and best practices for implementation.

The Importance of Autoscaling

Autoscaling serves multiple architectural objectives:

- **Elasticity**: Align resource allocation with real-time demand.

- **Cost Efficiency**: Pay only for what you use, avoiding over-provisioning.

- **Resilience**: Maintain application responsiveness during traffic spikes.

- **Operational Simplicity**: Reduce the need for manual scaling interventions.

Autoscaling can be reactive (based on metrics) or proactive (based on schedules or predictive models). Azure supports both approaches through different services.

Azure Autoscale for Virtual Machine Scale Sets

Virtual Machine Scale Sets (VMSS) are an IaaS solution that allows you to deploy and manage a group of identical VMs. Azure's built-in autoscaler monitors metrics like CPU usage and adjusts the number of instances accordingly.

Key Features

- Horizontal scaling (increase/decrease instance count)

- Integration with Azure Monitor metrics

- Scaling rules based on CPU, memory, disk IO, custom metrics

- Scheduled scaling for predictable workloads

CLI Example: Create a Scale Set with Autoscaling

```
az vmss create \
  --resource-group myResourceGroup \
  --name myScaleSet \
  --image UbuntuLTS \
  --upgrade-policy-mode automatic \
  --admin-username azureuser \
  --generate-ssh-keys \
  --instance-count 2

az monitor autoscale create \
  --resource-group myResourceGroup \
  --resource myScaleSet \
  --resource-type Microsoft.Compute/virtualMachineScaleSets \
  --name autoscaleSettings \
  --min-count 2 \
  --max-count 10 \
  --count 2

az monitor autoscale rule create \
  --resource-group myResourceGroup \
  --autoscale-name autoscaleSettings \
  --condition "Percentage CPU > 75 avg 5m" \
  --scale out 1
```

This configuration will scale out the VMSS by 1 instance if CPU usage exceeds 75% for 5 minutes.

Considerations

- Use **Availability Zones** to increase fault tolerance.

- Choose **custom images** if specialized configurations are needed.

- Monitor **startup times** to avoid scaling delays.

- Leverage **instance protection** to prevent termination of critical nodes.

Azure App Service Autoscaling

Azure App Service is a PaaS offering for web applications and APIs. It includes built-in autoscaling for App Service Plans in **Standard**, **Premium**, and **Isolated** tiers.

Scaling Rules

- Based on CPU, memory, HTTP queue length, custom metrics
- Time-based schedules for predictable demand
- WebJobs and background services support autoscaling with worker tiers

Portal Configuration Steps

1. Go to your App Service in Azure Portal.
2. Select "Scale out (App Service Plan)".
3. Add scale conditions based on a metric (e.g., CPU > 70%).
4. Set instance limits and cooldown intervals.

Best Practices

- Set **min** and **max** **instance** **count** to avoid runaway scaling.
- Use **slot swapping** for zero-downtime deployments alongside scaling.
- Combine autoscale with **Application Insights** for better telemetry feedback loops.

Azure Functions and Serverless Autoscaling

Azure Functions is a serverless compute service where autoscaling is **inherent** to the platform. In the **Consumption Plan**, Azure automatically scales the number of function instances based on incoming events.

Scaling Characteristics

- Millisecond cold-start for HTTP triggers (can be mitigated with Premium Plan)
- Unlimited instances (soft limits apply based on region and plan)
- Event-driven scaling with Azure Event Grid, Service Bus, HTTP, Timer, etc.

Use the Premium Plan or Dedicated Plan if you need:

- VNET   integration

- High-performance   requirements

- Long-running   executions   (>5   minutes)

Example: Consumption Plan Autoscale

You don't configure instance count for Functions in the Consumption Plan. Instead, focus on function runtime efficiency and concurrency control via host.json:

```json
{
  "functionTimeout": "00:05:00",
  "extensions": {
    "http": {
      "maxConcurrentRequests": 100
    }
  }
}
```

Event-Based Scaling Use Cases

- Real-time   file   processing   (Blob   triggers)

- Queue/message   processing   (Service   Bus,   Storage   Queues)

- Scheduled   jobs   (Timer   triggers)

Autoscaling with Azure Kubernetes Service (AKS)

AKS supports autoscaling both at the **cluster (node)** level and the **pod** level.

Cluster Autoscaler

- Automatically   adjusts   the   number   of   nodes   in   your   AKS   cluster.

- Works   by   monitoring   pending   pods   and   provisioning/removing   nodes.

Enable it via CLI:

```
az aks update \
  --resource-group myResourceGroup \
```

```
--name myAKSCluster \
--enable-cluster-autoscaler \
--min-count 1 \
--max-count 5
```

Horizontal Pod Autoscaler (HPA)

- Scales pods based on CPU/memory usage or custom metrics.

- Requires `metrics-server` to be installed.

Sample deployment with HPA:

```
apiVersion: autoscaling/v2
kind: HorizontalPodAutoscaler
metadata:
  name: myapp-hpa
spec:
  scaleTargetRef:
    apiVersion: apps/v1
    kind: Deployment
    name: myapp
  minReplicas: 2
  maxReplicas: 10
  metrics:
  - type: Resource
    resource:
      name: cpu
      target:
        type: Utilization
        averageUtilization: 70
```

KEDA for Event-Driven Scaling

KEDA (Kubernetes-based Event Driven Autoscaler) enables scaling based on event sources like queues or databases.

Use KEDA when:

- You want function-like scaling behavior in containers.

- Your workloads are event-heavy and bursty.

- You need integration with Service Bus, Kafka, or RabbitMQ.

Scheduled and Predictive Scaling

Azure Autoscale also supports **schedule-based rules**, useful for:

- Scaling down at night

- Scaling up during peak business hours

- Pre-warming capacity for scheduled events

Predictive autoscaling (preview feature) uses ML to forecast usage and scale ahead of time. This is especially valuable for predictable workloads like payroll runs or Monday traffic spikes.

Set a scheduled rule using CLI:

```
az monitor autoscale rule create \
  --autoscale-name myAutoScaleSetting \
  --resource-group myResourceGroup \
  --schedule \
  --recurrence 'Week' \
  --days 'Monday' \
  --time 08:00 \
  --scale out 2
```

Monitoring and Alerts for Autoscale

Monitoring autoscaling behavior is critical. You need visibility into:

- Instance counts over time

- Triggered scale actions

- Metrics leading to scale events

Use **Azure Monitor** and **Log Analytics**:

```
AzureDiagnostics
| where ResourceType == "AUTOSCALESETTINGS"
| project TimeGenerated, OperationName, ResultType, ResourceId
```

Set up alerts if:

- Scaling actions are throttled

- Scale-out fails due to quotas

- CPU/memory remains high despite scaling

Visualize scaling events on dashboards or embed them into Service Health monitoring.

Governance and Quotas

Autoscaling must be governed within defined boundaries:

- Set maximums to prevent cost overruns.

- Use **Azure Policy** to enforce limits on scale set size or SKU usage.

- Ensure role-based access control (RBAC) prevents unauthorized scale rule changes.

Example Policy to limit VMSS instance count:

```
{
  "if": {
    "allOf": [
      {
        "field": "type",
        "equals": "Microsoft.Compute/virtualMachineScaleSets"
      },
      {
        "field":
"Microsoft.Compute/virtualMachineScaleSets/sku.capacity",
        "greaterThan": 10
      }
    ]
  },
  "then": {
    "effect": "deny"
  }
}
```

Best Practices Summary

- **Design for statelessness**: Stateless apps scale more easily.

- **Use the right plan/tier**: Consumption for Functions, Premium for VNET support.

- **Set aggressive cooldowns**: Avoid oscillations from frequent scale events.

- **Benchmark and test**: Simulate load to validate autoscaling behavior.

- **Alert on failures**: Ensure autoscale doesn't silently fail.

- **Combine with caching/CDNs**: Reduce backend load and enhance responsiveness.

Conclusion

Autoscaling is a cornerstone of cloud-native design, enabling applications to respond fluidly to demand while maintaining cost and performance efficiency. Azure offers robust autoscaling capabilities across all compute models—from VMSS to App Services, AKS, and serverless functions.

By thoughtfully implementing autoscaling rules, using real-time telemetry, and aligning with architectural best practices, you ensure that your application is not only responsive but also resilient, efficient, and ready for growth.

In the next section, we'll dive into load balancing and traffic management strategies in Azure, exploring how to route, distribute, and secure incoming requests across your compute layers for high availability and performance.

Load Balancing and Traffic Management

Load balancing and traffic management are essential components in designing highly available, performant, and resilient cloud applications. As systems grow in scale and complexity, distributing traffic efficiently becomes critical to ensuring seamless user experiences, reducing latency, and mitigating failure domains. In Microsoft Azure, several services exist to manage load at different layers of the network stack—from basic IP-based load balancing to intelligent, application-aware global routing.

This section provides a comprehensive guide to load balancing and traffic distribution strategies in Azure. We will explore **Azure Load Balancer**, **Azure Application Gateway**, **Azure Front Door**, **Traffic Manager**, and related patterns for distributing traffic within and across regions, tiers, and endpoints.

Principles of Load Balancing

Effective load balancing aims to:

- **Distribute requests** across multiple servers to ensure no single server is overwhelmed

- **Improve performance** by serving users from the nearest or fastest backend

- **Increase availability** through redundancy and health probing

- **Enable horizontal scaling** of stateless services

- **Provide fault isolation** between application components

In Azure, load balancing decisions can be made based on:

- **Layer 4 (Transport Layer)** – TCP/UDP-based balancing (e.g., Azure Load Balancer)

- **Layer 7 (Application Layer)** – HTTP/HTTPS-based routing with path and host awareness (e.g., Application Gateway)

- **DNS-Based** – Global traffic distribution using DNS (e.g., Traffic Manager)

- **Anycast Routing** – Global presence with edge-based routing (e.g., Azure Front Door)

Azure Load Balancer

Azure Load Balancer is a high-performance, Layer 4 load balancer that distributes inbound traffic among healthy virtual machines within a virtual network. It supports both **public** and **internal** load balancing.

Key Features

- TCP/UDP protocol support

- Inbound NAT rules for port forwarding (e.g., RDP or SSH)

- Health probes for endpoint health

- High throughput and low latency

- Availability zone redundancy

Example: Creating a Basic Load Balancer

```
az network lb create \
  --name myLoadBalancer \
  --resource-group myResourceGroup \
  --sku Basic \
```

```
--frontend-ip-name myFrontEnd \
--backend-pool-name myBackEndPool \
--vnet-name myVNet
```

Add rules to distribute traffic:

```
az network lb rule create \
  --resource-group myResourceGroup \
  --lb-name myLoadBalancer \
  --name myHTTPRule \
  --protocol tcp \
  --frontend-port 80 \
  --backend-port 80 \
  --frontend-ip-name myFrontEnd \
  --backend-pool-name myBackEndPool \
  --probe-name myHealthProbe
```

Use **Standard SKU** for production workloads to take advantage of zone redundancy, HA ports, and better security.

Best Use Cases

- Load balancing TCP/UDP workloads (e.g., gaming, VoIP)

- Layer 4 backend services (e.g., custom APIs, microservices)

- Internal load balancing within VNet

Azure Application Gateway

Azure Application Gateway is a Layer 7 load balancer that provides intelligent HTTP/HTTPS traffic routing. It supports advanced features like **Web Application Firewall (WAF)**, **SSL termination**, **cookie-based session affinity**, and **path-based routing**.

Key Features

- SSL offloading

- URL-based routing

- Rewrite headers

- Autoscaling SKU

- WAF integration with OWASP rule sets

Example: Path-Based Routing

You can route /api/* to a microservice backend and /static/* to a static file store.

```
{
  "backendPools": [
    {
      "name": "apiBackend",
      "ipAddresses": ["10.0.0.10"]
    },
    {
      "name": "staticBackend",
      "ipAddresses": ["10.0.0.20"]
    }
  ],
  "routingRules": [
    {
      "name": "apiRoute",
      "paths": ["/api/*"],
      "backendPool": "apiBackend"
    },
    {
      "name": "staticRoute",
      "paths": ["/static/*"],
      "backendPool": "staticBackend"
    }
  ]
}
```

Set this up through ARM, Bicep, or Terraform scripts or through the portal interface.

Use Cases

- Hosting multi-tier web applications
- Secure routing of web traffic with integrated WAF
- Microservices architecture using path- or domain-based routing
- Centralized SSL termination

Azure Front Door

Azure Front Door is a global, scalable, secure entry point for delivering high-performance web applications. It combines global HTTP load balancing, SSL offloading, and content acceleration via Azure's edge network.

Key Features

- Anycast-based global routing
- Application layer security (WAF)
- URL path- and domain-based routing
- Session affinity and caching
- Health probes and automatic failover

Example: Routing by Geographic Location

You can direct users from Europe to the EU backend and users from the US to the US backend.

```
{
  "routingRules": [
    {
      "name": "geoBasedRouting",
      "patterns": ["/*"],
      "backendPools": {
        "Europe": "euBackend",
        "US": "usBackend"
      }
    }
  ]
}
```

Best Use Cases

- Global web applications
- High-performance APIs
- Multi-region failover with low-latency routing

- Combining   CDN   with   traffic   management

Front Door excels when you need **fast global access**, **dynamic failover**, and **layer 7 smart routing** at the edge.

Azure Traffic Manager

Azure Traffic Manager is a **DNS-based** traffic routing solution. It directs user requests to the most appropriate endpoint based on a routing method you choose.

Routing Methods

- **Priority**:   Always   routes   to   the   primary   unless   it   fails

- **Weighted**:   Distribute   traffic   proportionally   (e.g.,   70/30   split   for   A/B   testing)

- **Performance**:   Routes   based   on   lowest   network   latency

- **Geographic**:   Routes   based   on   user   location

- **Multivalue**:   Returns   multiple   endpoints   for   DNS   query

- **Subnet**:   Routes   based   on   source   IP   subnet

Example: Creating a Performance-Based Profile

```
az network traffic-manager profile create \
  --name myTrafficManager \
  --resource-group myResourceGroup \
  --routing-method Performance \
  --unique-dns-name mytmprofile \
  --ttl 30 \
  --monitor-path "/" \
  --monitor-port 80 \
  --monitor-protocol HTTP
```

Then add endpoints:

```
az network traffic-manager endpoint create \
  --name myEndpointEU \
  --profile-name myTrafficManager \
  --resource-group myResourceGroup \
  --type azureEndpoints \
  --target-resource-id /subscriptions/... \
```

```
--endpoint-location "West Europe"
```

Use Cases

- Distributing global traffic to regional Azure deployments

- DNS failover for disaster recovery

- Integrating with services hosted outside of Azure

- Lightweight global routing without content acceleration

Combined Patterns

Often, multiple load balancing layers are used together for advanced routing and failover strategies:

- **Front Door + Application Gateway**: Use Front Door for global routing and App Gateway for regional routing and WAF.

- **Traffic Manager + Load Balancer**: Use TM for DNS-based failover and Load Balancer for in-region traffic distribution.

- **Front Door + AKS Ingress Controller**: Front Door at the edge, with NGINX ingress inside AKS clusters.

These combinations allow fine-grained control over request flow, failover, and latency optimization.

Health Probes and Failover

Health probes determine if a backend is available and healthy. Most Azure load balancers allow configuration of:

- **Protocol** (HTTP, TCP)

- **Interval** and timeout

- **Unhealthy** thresholds

For instance, Front Door health probe configuration can specify:

- HTTP GET to /health

- Interval: 30 seconds

- Failover after 3 failures

When a probe fails, traffic is redirected to another backend automatically.

Security Considerations

- Use **NSGs and firewalls** to restrict public access to only through load balancers.

- **Terminate SSL** at App Gateway or Front Door to inspect traffic.

- Enable **Web Application Firewall** to mitigate OWASP Top 10 threats.

- Use **Private Link** with internal load balancers for backend security.

- Audit changes to routing rules using **Azure Monitor Activity Logs**.

Monitoring Load Balancers

Track metrics such as:

- **Backend** availability

- **Connection** count

- **HTTP** response codes

- **Throughput** and latency

Use **Log Analytics** and **Azure Monitor Workbooks** to visualize and alert on anomalies.

Sample KQL to identify failed probes:

```
AzureDiagnostics
| where ResourceType == "APPLICATIONGATEWAYS" and OperationName ==
"ApplicationGatewayProbeHealthStatus"
| where BackendHealthStatus == "Unhealthy"
| project TimeGenerated, BackendServerIPAddress, BackendHealthStatus
```

Best Practices

- Design for **failover and redundancy** at every layer.

- Use **zones and regions** to eliminate single points of failure.

- Implement **connection draining** to avoid breaking live sessions during scale-in.

- Configure **timeouts and retries** wisely in client apps.

- Document **routing rules and policies** for maintainability.

- Use **custom domains** and **HTTPS everywhere** for security and trust.

Conclusion

Load balancing and traffic management in Azure are not one-size-fits-all. Depending on your application's architecture, scale, and geographic requirements, you may need a combination of services like **Azure Load Balancer**, **Application Gateway**, **Traffic Manager**, and **Front Door**. Each serves a different layer and use case—from low-level transport to high-level application routing.

By carefully selecting and integrating these tools, architects can ensure applications are resilient, performant, scalable, and globally accessible. In the next section, we'll dive deeper into performance testing and tuning, helping you measure, validate, and improve the efficiency of your Azure workloads.

Performance Testing and Tuning

Performance testing and tuning are vital components of cloud architecture that ensure systems deliver optimal responsiveness, scalability, and stability under varying workloads. While Azure provides elastic resources, simply provisioning compute and storage is not enough—architects must validate that their applications and services perform efficiently under real-world conditions. Performance bottlenecks, inefficient resource usage, or configuration issues can undermine even the best cloud designs.

This section provides an in-depth exploration of performance testing methodologies, tools available in Azure, tuning techniques for common Azure services, and best practices for ensuring consistent and efficient performance in production environments.

Objectives of Performance Testing

Performance testing in Azure helps you answer critical questions such as:

- How many users can my application handle simultaneously?

- What is the latency of my APIs under heavy load?

- Which parts of my architecture become bottlenecks under stress?

- How do deployments affect performance?

- What configuration changes can reduce response times or improve throughput?

The key objectives of performance testing include:

- **Baseline Establishment**: Measure current performance for comparison over time.

- **Bottleneck Identification**: Detect inefficient code, database queries, or network delays.

- **Scalability Validation**: Ensure systems scale horizontally or vertically as intended.

- **Regression Detection**: Find performance regressions after code changes or deployments.

- **Optimization Guidance**: Use data to tune configurations, code, and infrastructure.

Types of Performance Testing

Different types of testing serve different purposes. Azure architects should be familiar with:

- **Load Testing**: Simulates expected usage patterns to verify system behavior.

- **Stress Testing**: Pushes the system beyond its limits to test failure handling.

- **Spike Testing**: Evaluates how the system responds to sudden increases in load.

- **Soak Testing**: Assesses stability over extended periods of sustained load.

- **Capacity Testing**: Determines the maximum load the system can handle without degradation.

Each test type reveals different insights and should be part of a broader performance validation strategy.

Tools for Performance Testing in Azure

Azure provides native and third-party tools for simulating load and analyzing performance.

Azure Load Testing

Azure Load Testing is a fully managed service that simulates high-scale load scenarios using Apache JMeter or custom scripts.

Key Features

- Managed infrastructure for test execution
- Real-time monitoring and telemetry
- Integration with Application Insights
- Automatic scaling of test engines
- Detailed reports with request-level metrics

Example: Creating a Load Test

```
az load test create \
  --resource-group myResourceGroup \
  --name myLoadTest \
  --load-test-resource myLoadTestResource \
  --description "API load test" \
  --test-plan ./loadtest.jmx
```

Test results can be streamed to Azure Monitor and Application Insights for correlation with backend metrics.

Apache JMeter

A popular open-source tool, JMeter is frequently used for load testing APIs and web apps. You can run it locally, in Azure VMs, or integrate it with Azure DevOps pipelines.

```
jmeter -n -t testplan.jmx -l results.jtl -e -o output-folder
```

k6

k6 is a developer-centric load testing tool written in JavaScript. It integrates well with CI/CD workflows and supports HTTP, WebSocket, and gRPC.

```
import http from 'k6/http';

export let options = {
  stages: [
    { duration: '30s', target: 50 },
    { duration: '1m', target: 200 },
    { duration: '10s', target: 0 },
  ],
};
```

```
export default function () {
  http.get('https://myapp.azurewebsites.net/api/data');
}
```

Run the test:

```
k6 run test.js
```

Application Insights for Performance Monitoring

Application Insights enables deep performance analysis of applications with out-of-the-box telemetry for:

- Request and dependency timings
- Exceptions and failures
- Custom events and performance counters
- Distributed tracing across services

Use the **Performance** tab in Application Insights to identify slow endpoints, measure response times, and view dependency trees.

Example Kusto Query: Slowest API Calls

```
requests
| where timestamp > ago(1h)
| where success == true
| order by duration desc
| take 10
```

This reveals which endpoints are performing poorly and need investigation.

Database Performance Tuning

Azure supports multiple databases (Azure SQL, Cosmos DB, PostgreSQL, etc.), each requiring tuning to avoid becoming a performance bottleneck.

Azure SQL Database

- Use **Query Performance Insight** to identify slow queries.
- Enable **Automatic Tuning** to apply indexes and force query plans.

- Monitor DTU/CPU/memory usage with **Metrics**.

Sample Query Tuning with Query Store

```
SELECT
    qs.query_id,
    qt.query_sql_text,
    rs.avg_duration,
    rs.execution_type_desc
FROM
    sys.query_store_query_text qt
JOIN
    sys.query_store_query qs ON qt.query_text_id = qs.query_text_id
JOIN
    sys.query_store_runtime_stats rs ON qs.query_id = rs.query_id
ORDER BY
    rs.avg_duration DESC;
```

Cosmos DB

- Partition your data strategically using a well-chosen partition key.

- Monitor **Request Units (RUs)** and scale throughput accordingly.

- Use **Indexing Policies** to avoid over-indexing large fields.

Networking and Caching Optimization

Performance isn't only about compute and database—it includes:

Azure CDN and Front Door

- Cache static content at edge locations

- Reduce latency for global users

- Offload traffic from backend servers

Azure Redis Cache

- Reduce database hits by caching frequently accessed data

- Store session data for stateful applications

- Implement pub/sub for fast message broadcasting

Example: Redis Set/Get in Python

```python
import redis
r = redis.StrictRedis(host='myredis.redis.cache.windows.net',
port=6380, db=0, ssl=True, password='myPassword')
r.set('key', 'value')
print(r.get('key'))
```

Implement intelligent caching strategies (e.g., write-through, time-based invalidation) to reduce response times significantly.

Compute Optimization Techniques

To get the best performance out of compute resources:

- Use **Premium SKUs** for latency-sensitive applications.

- Right-size VMs based on historical usage data.

- Enable **Autoscaling** with correct thresholds to prevent under/overprovisioning.

- For containers, ensure **resource limits** and **readiness probes** are configured.

Frontend Performance Tuning

Frontend latency impacts perceived performance. Improve client-side performance by:

- Enabling **GZIP compression** and **caching headers**

- Reducing HTTP request counts

- Using **Content Delivery Networks (CDN)** for static files

- Measuring performance with tools like **Lighthouse** or **Application Insights Availability Tests**

Example of setting a synthetic availability test:

```
az monitor app-insights web-test create \
  --name MyAvailabilityTest \
  --resource-group myResourceGroup \
  --location "East US" \
```

```
--kind ping \
--frequency 300 \
--timeout 30 \
--web-test-kind standard \
--configuration "{\"Url\":\"https://myapp.azurewebsites.net\"}"
```

Performance Regression Testing in CI/CD

Performance tests should be integrated into CI/CD pipelines to catch issues early.

Example with Azure DevOps Pipeline YAML:

```
- task: AzureLoadTest@1
  inputs:
    azureSubscription: 'MyServiceConnection'
    loadTestResource: 'myLoadTestResource'
    testId: 'loadtest1'
    testFile: 'loadtest.jmx'
```

Use performance thresholds to fail builds that introduce regressions:

```
- task: Bash@3
  inputs:
    targetType: 'inline'
    script: |
      if [ $(cat results.jtl | grep -c 'ResponseTime>2000') -gt 0 ];
then
        echo "Performance regression detected"
        exit 1
      fi
```

Best Practices for Performance Testing

- **Test in production-like environments** with realistic data and scale.

- **Use synthetic and real-user monitoring** for a complete picture.

- **Correlate telemetry** across layers—frontend, backend, database, network.

- **Automate performance tests** and run them frequently (e.g., nightly or per release).

- **Involve developers, DBAs, and network engineers** in tuning sessions.

- **Document test results** and track trends over time.

Conclusion

Performance testing and tuning are not one-time efforts but ongoing practices that ensure your cloud applications meet business expectations, deliver great user experiences, and scale predictably. Azure's ecosystem provides a comprehensive toolset for performance validation—from load testing and monitoring to telemetry analysis and infrastructure tuning.

By proactively identifying bottlenecks, integrating performance checks into CI/CD, and optimizing across compute, storage, and networking, architects can build Azure solutions that perform well under pressure and evolve with growing demand.

In the next section, we'll explore Azure Front Door and CDN services—critical tools for boosting application speed, availability, and global responsiveness.

Leveraging Azure Front Door and CDN

Delivering high-performance, highly available, and secure applications on a global scale requires careful attention to how traffic enters and flows through your infrastructure. Traditional server-centric architectures are no longer sufficient to meet the demands of modern digital experiences. Latency, fault tolerance, security, and intelligent routing all play crucial roles in delivering content effectively to users—regardless of where they are or what device they're using.

Azure provides two key services that help with optimizing content delivery and application performance across the globe: **Azure Front Door** and **Azure Content Delivery Network (CDN)**. Both services are designed to reduce latency, increase availability, and improve the user experience—but they serve slightly different purposes and operate at different layers of the stack.

This section dives deep into Azure Front Door and Azure CDN, exploring their architectures, use cases, configurations, and how they complement each other in a modern cloud solution.

Overview: Azure Front Door vs Azure CDN

Feature	Azure Front Door	Azure CDN
Layer	Layer 7 (HTTP/HTTPS)	Layer 7 (HTTP/HTTPS)
Primary Purpose	Global load balancing and app acceleration	Static content caching and acceleration

Routing Type	Anycast with intelligent routing	Caching from origin servers
Health Probes	Yes (Application-aware)	No
SSL Offloading	Yes	Yes
WAF Integration	Yes (built-in)	Yes (on premium tier)
Custom Rules	Path-based and header-based	Limited to CDN Rules Engine (Premium tier)
Dynamic Content	Yes (optimizes route to origin)	Not optimal (passes through to origin)
Static Content	Yes (pass-through or cached)	Yes (optimized for static assets)
Cost Model	Request and data transfer-based	Data transfer-based with caching

Front Door acts as an **application-aware global entry point**, while CDN is primarily for **optimizing the delivery of static content** like images, videos, and JavaScript bundles. However, when used together, they offer a powerful combination for speed, reliability, and scalability.

Azure Front Door: Global Application Delivery Network

Azure Front Door provides a modern edge-based architecture for **global HTTP/HTTPS load balancing**, **application acceleration**, and **smart routing**.

Core Features

- **Anycast-based global entry points** for fast DNS resolution
- **Split TCP and TLS termination at edge** for reduced latency
- **Layer 7 routing** based on URL path, hostname, and headers
- **Health probes** and failover between backend pools
- **Web Application Firewall (WAF)** integration with OWASP rule sets

- **Caching**   **for**   **static/dynamic**   **content**   (selectively   configurable)

- **Session**   **affinity**   via   cookies

Example: Routing Based on Path

You can create routing rules that direct /api/* traffic to one backend and /images/* to another:

```
{
  "routes": [
    {
      "name": "apiRoute",
      "patterns": ["/api/*"],
      "backendPool": "apiBackend"
    },
    {
      "name": "imageRoute",
      "patterns": ["/images/*"],
      "backendPool": "cdnBackend"
    }
  ]
}
```

This supports microservice architectures and performance optimization at the edge.

Health Probes and Failover

Each backend pool in Front Door is associated with a health probe. If a backend becomes unhealthy, traffic is automatically routed to a healthy region, improving availability.

Example of configuration:

- Probe   path: /health

- Interval: 30   seconds

- Method: GET

- Expected   status   codes: 200–399

Azure CDN: Accelerating Static Content

Azure CDN caches content close to users at **global edge nodes**. This reduces latency and load on your backend services.

Azure offers several CDN providers under its umbrella:

- **Azure CDN Standard from Microsoft**

- **Azure CDN Standard from Akamai**

- **Azure CDN Standard/Premium from Verizon**

Key Features

- Caching of images, videos, CSS, JavaScript

- Origin pull from Azure Storage, App Services, or custom origins

- Rules Engine (Premium tiers) for header rewrites, URL redirects

- Custom domain and SSL support

- Cache purging and time-to-live (TTL) control

- Geo-filtering and IP-based blocking

Example: Create CDN Endpoint for Blob Storage

```
az cdn profile create \
  --name myCDNProfile \
  --resource-group myResourceGroup \
  --sku Standard_Microsoft

az cdn endpoint create \
  --name myCDNEndpoint \
  --profile-name myCDNProfile \
  --resource-group myResourceGroup \
  --origin mystorageaccount.blob.core.windows.net \
  --origin-host-header mystorageaccount.blob.core.windows.net
```

Files stored in Blob Storage can now be served globally with low latency.

Combined Use Case: Front Door + CDN

For optimal performance:

- Use **Front Door** as the **global application entry point**

- Route static asset paths to **CDN endpoints**

- Use **backend pools** for API or dynamic routes (App Services, AKS, etc.)

- Configure **custom domain with SSL** on Front Door for all traffic

- Implement **WAF policies** for security

Routing configuration might look like:

```
{
  "routes": [
    {
      "name": "staticRoute",
      "patterns": ["/static/*"],
      "backendPool": "azureCDN"
    },
    {
      "name": "appRoute",
      "patterns": ["/*"],
      "backendPool": "aksCluster"
    }
  ]
}
```

This setup gives you edge-based acceleration, intelligent routing, and centralized management.

Performance Benefits

Both Front Door and CDN reduce latency through:

- **Anycast routing**: Minimizes DNS lookup and routing time

- **Edge caching**: Serves content from nearby nodes

- **TLS termination**: Reduces compute load on backend services

- **Connection reuse**: Keeps TCP sessions alive at the edge

- **Reduced backend hops**: Limits origin fetches to cache misses

Together, they significantly improve **Time To First Byte (TTFB)** and reduce **round-trip times** for global users.

Security Integration

Azure Front Door offers built-in **Web Application Firewall (WAF)** capabilities:

- Protects against SQL Injection, XSS, and other OWASP vulnerabilities

- Custom rule sets with IP blocking, geo-fencing, bot protection

- Integration with Microsoft Threat Intelligence feeds

CDN Premium also supports WAF through integration with partner platforms (e.g., Akamai or Verizon).

Best practices:

- Always enable **HTTPS-only** access

- Use **custom domains with managed certificates**

- Combine WAF with **rate limiting** and **threat detection**

- Leverage **IP allow/block lists** and geo filters

Logging and Analytics

Azure Front Door and CDN integrate with **Azure Monitor**, **Log Analytics**, and **Diagnostic Settings**.

Enable diagnostics:

```
az network front-door diagnostics create \
  --resource-group myResourceGroup \
  --front-door-name myFrontDoor \
  --enabled true \
  --log-analytics-workspace <workspace-id>
```

Track metrics such as:

- **Cache** **hit/miss** **ratio**

- **Origin** **fetch** **time**

- **Latency** **distribution**

- **Response** **size** **and** **status** **codes**

Use **Kusto Query Language (KQL)** in Log Analytics to detect anomalies, slow responses, or DDoS activity.

CI/CD and Infrastructure as Code

Front Door and CDN configurations should be treated as **infrastructure-as-code** using tools like:

- **ARM** **Templates**

- **Bicep**

- **Terraform**

- **Azure** **CLI** **and** **PowerShell**

Example: Terraform module for Front Door

```
resource "azurerm_frontdoor" "main" {
  name                = "myFrontDoor"
  resource_group_name = azurerm_resource_group.main.name
  location            = "global"

  frontend_endpoints {
    name                          = "myFE"
    host_name                     = "myapp.azurefd.net"
    session_affinity_enabled      = true
    session_affinity_ttl_seconds  = 100
    web_application_firewall_policy_link_id                  =
azurerm_frontdoor_firewall_policy.main.id
  }
```

```
backend_pools {
  name = "primary"
  backends {
    address = "myapp.azurewebsites.net"
    http_port  = 80
    https_port = 443
  }
}
}
```

This ensures repeatability and version control of your edge infrastructure.

Best Practices

- Use **Front Door** for **dynamic content** and **failover**
- Use **CDN** for **static content delivery**
- Implement **cache-control headers** in your applications
- Configure **automatic certificate renewal** for custom domains
- Segment routes with **path-** and **domain-based routing**
- Regularly purge outdated CDN content for consistency
- Test failover scenarios with disabled backend health probes

Conclusion

Azure Front Door and CDN form a critical part of high-performance, global application delivery strategies. When properly implemented, they reduce latency, improve throughput, protect against threats, and optimize content distribution. These services shift performance and reliability responsibilities to the edge—closer to your users—and decouple them from your origin infrastructure.

Whether you're building a single-region startup site or a globally distributed enterprise application, leveraging Front Door and CDN provides a scalable, resilient foundation for modern web architecture. In the next chapter, we'll shift our focus toward resilience and high availability, exploring how to architect for failure in a cloud-native world.

100 |

Chapter 4: Building Resilient and Highly Available Systems

Understanding Fault Domains and Update Domains

In cloud architecture, the ability to withstand failure and maintain availability is paramount. Modern applications must be designed with the assumption that failure is inevitable—be it hardware, software, or network components. Azure addresses these realities with architectural patterns and infrastructure design elements that promote resilience, fault isolation, and service continuity.

Two foundational constructs that support high availability in Azure are **Fault Domains** and **Update Domains**. Understanding how these domains function and how to design for them enables architects to minimize the blast radius of hardware failures and maintenance events, thus maintaining application uptime and integrity.

What Are Fault Domains?

A **Fault Domain (FD)** is a grouping of Azure resources that share a common power source and network switch. In simpler terms, a fault domain represents a physical rack of servers within a data center. If the rack experiences a failure—such as a power outage or hardware issue—**all resources in that fault domain** could become unavailable.

Azure places resources into separate fault domains to ensure that a failure does not affect all instances of a service.

Key Characteristics

- Fault domains isolate **hardware** and **power infrastructure**.

- Each Azure region has a specific number of supported fault domains (typically 2 or 3).

- Fault domains are particularly important for **IaaS workloads** (Virtual Machines, VM Scale Sets).

Real-World Analogy

Imagine a data center with racks A, B, and C. If Rack A loses power, only VMs in Rack A are affected. VMs in Racks B and C continue operating. By spreading your VMs across racks, you limit the scope of impact.

What Are Update Domains?

An **Update Domain (UD)** is a logical grouping of Azure resources used for **sequential software or platform updates**. When Azure applies updates—such as OS patches or hypervisor upgrades—it does so one update domain at a time. This approach ensures that not all resources are updated simultaneously, minimizing downtime.

Key Characteristics

- Update domains provide **software fault isolation**.

- Azure ensures that only one update domain is rebooted at a time.

- By default, Azure supports **5 update domains**, but this can be increased to **20** for larger scale sets.

- Update domains are spread **within fault domains**, offering layered fault tolerance.

Real-World Analogy

Think of update domains like rotating restaurant shifts. If a server needs a break, others continue to serve guests. Similarly, if one update domain is under maintenance, others continue to serve traffic.

Azure Availability Sets

An **Availability Set** is an Azure construct that helps you distribute VMs across **multiple fault and update domains**. It ensures that at least one VM instance remains operational during:

- Planned maintenance (e.g., host patching)

- Unplanned downtime (e.g., power failure)

Default Configuration

- 2 or 3 Fault Domains (region-specific)

- 5 Update Domains (default, configurable up to 20)

Example: Creating an Availability Set via CLI

```
az vm availability-set create \
  --name myAvailabilitySet \
  --resource-group myResourceGroup \
```

```
--platform-fault-domain-count 3 \
--platform-update-domain-count 5 \
--location eastus
```

When deploying VMs:

```
az vm create \
  --resource-group myResourceGroup \
  --name vm1 \
  --availability-set myAvailabilitySet \
  --image UbuntuLTS \
  --admin-username azureuser \
  --generate-ssh-keys
```

Each VM added to the set will be automatically assigned to different update and fault domains.

Impact on SLA

Azure offers **99.95% SLA** for VMs within an availability set. This translates to approximately **22 minutes of downtime per month**. In contrast, a single VM without availability protection offers **99.9% SLA** (about 43 minutes of downtime monthly).

For **mission-critical workloads**, placing VMs into availability sets or zones is not optional—it's a **requirement for high availability**.

Application Design Implications

Designing for domain-aware high availability goes beyond infrastructure. Applications must be aware of how they scale and recover from failure. Consider the following:

- **Stateless Services**: Deploy stateless services across multiple update and fault domains to allow any instance to take over if another fails.

- **Session Persistence**: Use distributed caches like Azure Redis or external session stores to avoid binding sessions to a single instance.

- **Graceful Shutdown and Retry Logic**: Ensure services can handle instance restarts gracefully.

- **Health Probes and Load Balancing**: Load balancers should route only to healthy instances across fault/update domains.

Domain Behavior in VM Scale Sets

Azure **Virtual Machine Scale Sets (VMSS)** also support fault and update domains, particularly in **flexible orchestration mode**.

Key Points

- VMSS with flexible orchestration distributes VMs across **fault and update domains**, similar to availability sets.

- Autoscaling respects domain distribution to prevent hotspots.

- Use **proximity placement groups** to minimize latency while retaining fault domain awareness.

Availability Zones vs. Fault/Update Domains

While fault and update domains provide **intra-datacenter redundancy**, **Availability Zones (AZs)** offer **inter-datacenter redundancy**.

Feature	Fault Domains	Availability Zones
Redundancy Level	Within a datacenter	Across datacenters in a region
Purpose	Protect against rack failure	Protect against entire datacenter failure
Configuration	Via Availability Sets	Via zonal services or zone-aware VMs
SLA	99.95% (VMs in availability sets)	99.99% (VMs across AZs)

For higher fault isolation, consider using both strategies together:

- Use **Availability Zones** to protect across buildings.

- Use **Availability Sets** to protect within a zone.

Monitoring and Alerting

It's important to monitor the health of each VM instance and be alerted if an entire fault or update domain becomes unavailable.

Key Metrics

- VM availability per domain

- Platform updates or reboot events

- Resource health events from Azure Resource Health

Sample Alert Rule Using Azure Monitor

```
az monitor metrics alert create \
  --name "VMUnavailabilityAlert" \
  --resource-group myResourceGroup \
  --scopes                              "/subscriptions/<sub-
id>/resourceGroups/myResourceGroup/providers/Microsoft.Compute/virtu
alMachines/vm1" \
  --condition "avg Percentage CPU < 1" \
  --window-size 5m \
  --evaluation-frequency 1m \
  --action-group myActionGroup
```

This alert can signal if a VM is underutilized—often an indicator of failure.

Limitations and Considerations

- Not all Azure services support availability sets (e.g., PaaS services).

- Availability sets must be configured **at the time of VM creation** and **cannot be changed** **later**.

- Costs are slightly higher due to the need to provision multiple VMs.

- Application redundancy logic must complement infrastructure-level redundancy.

Best Practices

- Always deploy **at least two instances** of critical services into an availability set or zone.

- Use **managed disks**, which are zone-aware and fault-tolerant.

- Configure **load balancers** to distribute traffic across domains.

- Use **shared image galleries** for VM provisioning consistency.

- Automate updates using **Azure Update Management** while respecting update domains.

Conclusion

Understanding and properly utilizing **fault domains** and **update domains** is essential for any Azure architect aiming to build resilient, enterprise-grade solutions. While they operate behind the scenes, their impact on application uptime and maintainability is significant. Combined with availability sets, load balancing, and sound application architecture, these domains help ensure your systems can withstand failures—planned or unplanned—without impacting user experience or business continuity.

In the next section, we'll extend this foundation by exploring how **geo-redundancy** and **disaster recovery** planning contribute to broader business continuity strategies in Azure.

Geo-Redundancy and Disaster Recovery

Ensuring business continuity in the face of regional outages, natural disasters, or catastrophic failures requires more than local redundancy—it demands **geo-redundant architectures** and comprehensive **disaster recovery (DR) strategies**. While Azure's infrastructure offers high availability through Availability Sets and Zones, true resilience at a global scale comes from distributing workloads and data across geographically distinct regions.

This section explores Azure's geo-redundancy capabilities, outlines disaster recovery patterns and services, and provides practical guidance on building systems that can recover quickly and continue functioning when faced with significant disruptions.

Understanding Geo-Redundancy

Geo-redundancy refers to the practice of replicating applications, services, and data across multiple Azure regions. The goal is to isolate workloads from region-specific failures and ensure continuity of operations in extreme scenarios.

Benefits of Geo-Redundancy

- Protection from entire region outages

- Seamless failover to alternate regions

- Compliance with regulatory requirements (e.g., cross-region backup)

- Enhanced SLA commitments for mission-critical systems

Azure offers **paired regions**, which are region pairs within the same geography (e.g., UK South and UK West) that provide platform-managed replication and updates staggered to reduce downtime risks.

Azure Paired Regions

Every Azure region is paired with another within the same geography to support geo-redundancy. Azure ensures:

- **Region updates are sequenced**: Only one region in the pair is updated at a time.

- **Automatic replication** for some services (e.g., Geo-Redundant Storage).

- **Availability in paired regions** for backup and disaster recovery services.

Examples of Region Pairs

- East US ↔ West US

- North Europe ↔ West Europe

- Southeast Asia ↔ East Asia

- UK South ↔ UK West

Designing with region pairs ensures optimal replication support and faster recovery during outages.

Disaster Recovery Strategy in Azure

A robust disaster recovery plan in Azure is based on the **four R's**:

1. **Replication** – Keep data and configurations synchronized between primary and secondary regions.

2. **Recovery Point Objective (RPO)** – Maximum data loss (measured in time) tolerated.

3. **Recovery Time Objective (RTO)** – Time required to bring a system back online.

4. **Redirection** – Traffic routing to secondary regions upon failover.

These objectives guide the selection of services and architecture. For mission-critical applications, aim for **low RPO/RTO** with near-real-time replication and automation.

Azure Services Supporting Geo-Redundancy

Azure provides a variety of services and tools to enable cross-region replication and recovery.

Azure Site Recovery (ASR)

Azure Site Recovery automates disaster recovery for VMs, physical servers, and workloads. It enables:

- Cross-region replication of VMs (Windows and Linux)

- Application-consistent snapshots

- Custom recovery plans

- Test failover without impact on production

Example: Enable Replication

```
az backup protection enable-for-vm \
  --resource-group myResourceGroup \
  --vault-name myRecoveryVault \
  --vm myVM \
  --policy-name DefaultPolicy
```

Use the Azure Portal or PowerShell for complete recovery plan automation, including app-tier sequencing and custom scripts.

Azure Backup

Azure Backup supports geo-redundant storage (GRS) by default, ensuring that backups are replicated to a secondary Azure region. Backup supports:

- VMs

- SQL   Server,   SAP   HANA

- Azure   File   Shares

- Blob   storage

For increased durability, opt for **GRS** over **LRS** when configuring vaults:

```
az backup vault create \
  --name myBackupVault \
  --resource-group myResourceGroup \
  --location eastus \
  --sku Standard
```

Ensure policies are defined for regular backups and long-term retention (e.g., 10 years for compliance).

Geo-Redundant Storage (GRS and RA-GRS)

Azure Storage accounts offer multiple replication options:

- **LRS (Locally Redundant Storage)** – 3 replicas in a single region

- **ZRS (Zone-Redundant Storage)** – 3 replicas across availability zones

- **GRS (Geo-Redundant Storage)** – LRS in primary + asynchronous replication to paired region

- **RA-GRS (Read-Access GRS)** – Same as GRS but with read-access to the secondary region

Choose GRS or RA-GRS for backups, long-term data storage, or mission-critical workloads.

```
az storage account create \
  --name mystorageaccount \
  --resource-group myResourceGroup \
  --location eastus \
  --sku Standard_GRS \
```

```
--kind StorageV2
```

Monitor **replication status** using storage metrics and alerts.

Cosmos DB Global Distribution

Cosmos DB natively supports multi-region writes and reads. You can:

- Enable **automatic** **failover**
- Route traffic based on latency
- Design for **five** **9's** (99.999%) availability

```
az cosmosdb update \
  --name myCosmosDB \
  --resource-group myResourceGroup \
  --locations regionName=westus failoverPriority=0 \
               regionName=eastus failoverPriority=1
```

Cosmos DB is ideal for globally distributed applications needing low-latency access to data across geographies.

Traffic Routing for Disaster Recovery

Once your services are replicated across regions, traffic must be intelligently routed during failover. Azure offers several options:

Azure Traffic Manager

- **DNS-based** routing
- Failover, performance, or geographic routing modes
- Works across Azure and non-Azure endpoints

Example: Create a Failover Profile

```
az network traffic-manager profile create \
  --name myTMProfile \
  --resource-group myResourceGroup \
```

```
--routing-method Failover \
--unique-dns-name myapp-tm \
--monitor-path "/" \
--monitor-port 80 \
--monitor-protocol HTTP
```

Azure Front Door

- Edge-based   HTTP   global   routing

- Integrated   with   health   probes   and   WAF

- Supports   automatic   regional   failover   and   fast   TTL   updates

Front Door provides more seamless routing for **web applications** than Traffic Manager, especially under HTTPS and low-latency requirements.

Application Design for Disaster Recovery

High availability requires application logic that complements infrastructure-level redundancy.

Best practices:

- **Statelessness**: Minimize local dependencies and use shared or replicated data stores.

- **Configuration Management**: Store environment configs in shared key-value stores like   Azure   App   Configuration   or   Key   Vault.

- **Eventual Consistency**: Accept that some delays may exist in replication between regions.

- **Testing and Validation**: Regularly test failover plans and validate data recovery times.

Use **Chaos Engineering** principles—like simulating region outages—to validate the robustness of your DR plans.

Automation and Testing

Disaster recovery should not be manual. Automate:

- Resource provisioning using ARM, Bicep, or Terraform

- Replication and backup using Azure Policies and blueprints

- Traffic failover using scripts or Azure Runbooks

Test your plan with:

```
az backup recoverypoint list \
  --vault-name myBackupVault \
  --resource-group myResourceGroup \
  --container-name myContainer \
  --item-name myVM
```

Restore using test mode to validate recovery without affecting production.

Regulatory and Compliance Considerations

Certain industries and jurisdictions require specific data residency and recovery strategies. Ensure that:

- Backup and recovery meet **ISO 27001**, **HIPAA**, **GDPR**, and local laws.

- Replication does not violate **cross-border data transfer restrictions**.

- All disaster recovery runbooks are **documented and reviewed**.

Use **Azure Policy** to enforce geo-redundant configurations across subscriptions and resources.

Cost Considerations

Geo-redundancy adds cost but is often outweighed by the potential losses of unavailability. Evaluate:

- **Storage replication costs** (GRS vs. LRS)

- **Secondary region resource costs** (active-active vs. warm standby)

- **Traffic routing and DNS updates**

- **Automation and operational testing tools**

Use **Azure Cost Management** to model and track cross-region expenditures.

Conclusion

Geo-redundancy and disaster recovery are essential for protecting applications and data against regional failures. Azure provides an extensive toolkit—from Site Recovery and Traffic Manager to GRS storage and globally distributed databases—to build and automate resilient systems.

Disaster recovery isn't just about infrastructure—it's a mindset, a discipline, and a continuous process. By architecting with region-pair awareness, enabling automated replication, and rigorously testing failover, architects can ensure their solutions remain operational even in the face of significant disruptions.

In the next section, we will explore how **Availability Zones and Availability Sets** provide further depth to Azure's high availability capabilities—helping to build robust systems that endure both hardware and datacenter-level failures.

Azure Availability Zones and Sets

Resilience in cloud architecture requires a deep understanding of how infrastructure is distributed and protected across physical and logical boundaries. In Azure, **Availability Zones (AZs)** and **Availability Sets** are two critical mechanisms that ensure high availability and fault tolerance. While Availability Sets offer protection within a single data center, Availability Zones provide datacenter-level isolation, giving you the tools to architect robust, multi-tier, highly available services that can withstand a wide range of failures.

This section examines Availability Zones and Sets in detail, comparing their purposes, configurations, best practices, and when to use each in your architecture. These constructs are vital for any solution where uptime, consistency, and redundancy are top priorities.

Understanding Availability Zones

Availability Zones are physically separate locations within an Azure region. Each zone is made up of one or more datacenters equipped with independent power, cooling, and networking. These zones are connected through high-speed, low-latency networks and are designed to be resilient to datacenter-level failures.

Key Characteristics

- Each Azure region with zone support has at least three Availability Zones.

- Zones are isolated from one another physically and logically.

- Services deployed across zones can achieve **99.99%** **SLA**.

- Zone-redundant services automatically replicate across zones.

Benefits

- High   fault   isolation

- Automatic   traffic   rerouting

- Greater   redundancy   than   Availability   Sets

- Critical   for   financial,   healthcare,   and   compliance-sensitive   workloads

Examples of Zone-Aware Regions

- East   US   2

- Central   US

- West   Europe

- UK   South

- Southeast   Asia

To verify zone support:

```
az vm list-skus \
  --location eastus2 \
  --output table
```

Look for zoneDetails in the output.

Deploying to Availability Zones

When deploying VMs, storage, or other resources, you can specify the zone explicitly. Each zone is represented by an integer: 1, 2, or 3.

```
az vm create \
  --resource-group myResourceGroup \
  --name myZoneVM \
  --image UbuntuLTS \
  --zone 1 \
  --admin-username azureuser \
  --generate-ssh-keys
```

You can create multiple instances in different zones and use a **load balancer** to distribute traffic across them.

```
az network lb create \
  --resource-group myResourceGroup \
  --name myZonalLB \
  --sku Standard \
  --frontend-ip-name myFrontEnd \
  --backend-pool-name myBackEndPool
```

Standard SKU is required for zone-aware deployments.

Zone-Redundant Services

Many Azure services are **natively zone-redundant**, meaning Azure handles replication across zones for you:

- **Azure SQL Database** (Business Critical tier)
- **Azure Kubernetes Service** (AKS)
- **Azure Load Balancer** (Standard)
- **Azure App Service** (Premium v2/v3)
- **Azure Cosmos DB**
- **Azure Storage** (ZRS)

When using zone-redundant SKUs, you don't need to manually manage the zone assignment—the platform handles fault tolerance.

Example: Zone-Redundant Storage

```
az storage account create \
```

```
--name mystorageaccount \
--resource-group myResourceGroup \
--location eastus2 \
--sku Standard_ZRS \
--kind StorageV2
```

This ensures that your data is automatically replicated across zones without requiring custom logic or failover handling.

Availability Sets

An **Availability Set** is a logical grouping of VMs that allows Azure to distribute them across **multiple fault domains and update domains** within a single datacenter.

Characteristics

- Provides 99.95% SLA

- Isolates VMs from both power/network failures (fault domains) and maintenance events (update domains)

- Supports up to 3 fault domains and up to 20 update domains

- Must be defined at **VM creation time**

Use Cases

- Applications with multiple VMs that run in the same region without the need for zone distribution

- Legacy applications that are not zone-aware

- Workloads where proximity (e.g., low latency within a rack) matters more than fault tolerance across zones

Example: Create Availability Set

```
az vm availability-set create \
  --name myAvailabilitySet \
  --resource-group myResourceGroup \
  --platform-fault-domain-count 2 \
  --platform-update-domain-count 5
```

Add VMs into the availability set:

```
az vm create \
  --resource-group myResourceGroup \
  --name myAppVM1 \
  --availability-set myAvailabilitySet \
  --image UbuntuLTS \
  --admin-username azureuser \
  --generate-ssh-keys
```

Comparing Availability Zones and Availability Sets

Feature	Availability Zones	Availability Sets
Fault Isolation	Datacenter level	Rack level
SLA	99.99%	99.95%
Scope	Region-wide	Single datacenter
Use Case	Critical services needing zone fault tolerance	Multi-VM apps requiring maintenance isolation
Configuration	Zone parameter on resource	Availability set parameter on VM
Zonal Resource Support	Requires supported SKUs and region	Broad VM support
Dependency	Zone-enabled regions only	Available in all regions

Key takeaway: Use **Availability Zones** when high availability and disaster isolation are paramount. Use **Availability Sets** when you're constrained to a single datacenter or using non-zonal services.

Application Design Considerations

To fully benefit from zone- or set-based distribution, your application must be architected for redundancy.

Best Practices

- Design for **statelessness** whenever possible.

- Use **externalized state** (e.g., Azure SQL, Redis, Blob Storage) to allow failover between zones.

- Implement **retry policies** in client apps to handle transient failures.

- Avoid hard-coding IPs or endpoints—use load balancers and DNS.

- Ensure **autoscaling** is enabled across zone-aware resource pools.

- Monitor zone-based metrics to detect skew or imbalance in usage.

High Availability Patterns Using AZs

Pattern: Zonal Load Balancing

- Deploy three instances of your web app in three different zones.

- Place them behind an **Azure Load Balancer (Standard)**.

- Configure health probes to monitor VM availability.

- Achieve 99.99% availability even if one zone fails.

Pattern: Zone-Redundant Services

- Use **Azure SQL Database** in Business Critical tier with zone-redundant HA.

- Use **Azure App Service Premium v3** with zone redundancy enabled.

- Simplify operations by relying on Azure-managed HA across zones.

Pattern: Multi-Region + AZ

- Combine **Availability Zones** with **Geo-Redundancy**.

- Primary deployment: VM instances across AZs in East US 2.

- Secondary deployment: Failover to another region (e.g., Central US).

- Use **Traffic Manager** or **Front Door** for routing.

Monitoring and Alerts

Track zone-specific failures or performance issues with **Azure Monitor**:

- Use **Activity Logs** to view zone outages or maintenance.
- Monitor **VM status** and **load balancer probe failures**.
- Create **availability dashboards** to track uptime by zone.

KQL Example: VM Availability by Zone

```
Heartbeat
| summarize count() by bin(TimeGenerated, 5m), Computer, ResourceId,
Location
```

Alert on missing heartbeats from one zone to detect systemic issues.

Infrastructure as Code (IaC) for Zones and Sets

Use Bicep, ARM, or Terraform to automate deployments and enforce availability best practices.

Example: Terraform for Zonal VM

```
resource "azurerm_linux_virtual_machine" "vm" {
  name                = "myvm"
  resource_group_name = azurerm_resource_group.rg.name
  location            = azurerm_resource_group.rg.location
  zone                = "2"

  size                = "Standard_DS2_v2"
  ...
}
```

Versioning your infrastructure enables repeatable, reliable deployment of HA configurations.

Conclusion

Availability Zones and Availability Sets are essential tools for designing resilient, fault-tolerant applications on Azure. While zones provide stronger fault isolation at the datacenter level, sets remain useful for legacy workloads and environments where zonal deployment isn't available.

By leveraging these capabilities effectively—and combining them with smart application architecture, load balancing, and monitoring—you ensure your systems are prepared to handle failures gracefully, deliver consistent user experiences, and meet stringent uptime SLAs.

In the next section, we'll explore how to design comprehensive **failover and backup** strategies that complement availability planning and provide safety nets for data integrity and operational continuity.

Designing for Failover and Backup

Designing for failover and backup is a critical responsibility for any cloud architect. While high availability ensures minimal disruption during localized failures, **failover** provides continuity during broader outages, and **backup** ensures data durability in the event of corruption, deletion, or compromise. These mechanisms are the cornerstone of a resilient cloud strategy, especially in the face of unexpected outages, system misconfigurations, and data loss events.

This section explores architectural patterns, Azure-native services, automation techniques, and best practices for implementing robust failover and backup strategies. The goal is to ensure that when something goes wrong—and eventually, it will—your systems can recover quickly, accurately, and with minimal data loss.

Principles of Failover Design

Failover is the automatic or manual switching of services from a primary system or component to a secondary one during a failure. In Azure, failover applies to compute, networking, databases, storage, and entire application stacks.

Types of Failover

- **Application-level Failover** – Redirecting user traffic to a healthy instance or region.

- **Database Failover** – Switching to a replicated database node.

- **Infrastructure Failover** – Moving VMs or containers to alternative hosts or zones.

- **Manual Failover** – Triggered by administrators (less ideal for mission-critical workloads).

- **Automatic Failover** – Built into services or orchestrated using logic and probes.

Key Attributes of Effective Failover

- **Speed** (low Recovery Time Objective)

- **Minimal Data Loss** (low Recovery Point Objective)

- **Automation** to reduce human error

- **Observability** for quick detection and response

Azure Services That Enable Failover

Azure provides several managed services with built-in failover support or features that can be orchestrated to achieve seamless failover.

Azure Front Door

- Global load balancer with health probes and automatic failover.

- Routes traffic to the healthiest endpoint across regions.

- Use **Priority-based routing** to establish primary/secondary failover targets.

```
az network front-door backend-pool update \
  --front-door-name myFrontDoor \
  --resource-group myRG \
  --name myBackendPool \
  --priority 1
```

Failover is automatic based on probe health.

Azure Traffic Manager

- DNS-based routing.

- Failover, weighted, and performance routing.

- Suitable for hybrid and multi-cloud environments.

```
az network traffic-manager profile create \
```

```
--name myProfile \
--resource-group myRG \
--routing-method Failover \
--unique-dns-name myapp-tm \
--monitor-protocol HTTP \
--monitor-path "/health"
```

Assign endpoints and monitor readiness using HTTP probes.

Azure SQL Database Auto-Failover Groups

- Enables automatic cross-region failover.

- Supports multiple databases within a failover group.

- Provides readable secondary replicas.

```
az sql failover-group create \
  --name myFailoverGroup \
  --partner-server mySecondaryServer \
  --resource-group myRG \
  --server myPrimaryServer \
  --failover-policy Automatic \
  --grace-period 1
```

Applications connect via a failover group listener that abstracts primary/secondary switches.

Designing for Stateful and Stateless Failover

Failover strategies differ based on the **statefulness** of components.

Stateless Components

- Easier to fail over.

- Examples: Web apps, API gateways, microservices.

- Best Practice: Deploy to multiple zones/regions and load balance globally.

Stateful Components

- Require data synchronization or replication.

- Examples: Databases, file systems, message queues.

- Best Practice: Use managed services with built-in replication (e.g., Cosmos DB, Azure SQL, Storage with RA-GRS).

Combine these elements to create end-to-end continuity:

Component	Failover Approach
App Service	Slot-based deployment + Front Door
VMs	Availability Zones + Site Recovery
Databases	Auto-failover groups or geo-replication
Storage	RA-GRS or ZRS + Lifecycle rules
Identity	Azure AD with multi-region fallback

Backup Strategy Essentials

Backup is the process of capturing a snapshot of data or configuration to restore from in the event of loss or corruption. While failover handles uptime, backup handles **data integrity and continuity**.

Backup Targets

- Virtual Machines (disks)

- Azure SQL Database

- Azure Files and Blobs

- On-premises servers (via MARS or DPM)

- Kubernetes clusters (using third-party tools like Velero)

Backup Retention and Policy Design

Design policies that balance **data retention**, **compliance**, and **cost**:

- Daily backups retained for 7–30 days.

- Weekly full backups retained for 3–12 months.

- Yearly compliance snapshots for 7–10 years (or more).

Use **Azure Backup Policies** to enforce these rules:

```
az backup policy create \
  --resource-group myRG \
  --vault-name myVault \
  --name myPolicy \
  --backup-management-type AzureIaasVM \
  --policy "{...JSON settings...}"
```

Define frequency, retention ranges, and time windows.

Azure Backup Vault and Recovery Services

Azure Backup uses **Recovery Services Vaults** and **Backup Vaults** to manage backups.

Key Features

- Encryption at rest

- Geo-redundant or locally redundant storage options

- Soft-delete and multi-user authorization

- Alerts and monitoring integration

Example: Enable VM protection

```
az backup protection enable-for-vm \
  --vm myVM \
  --vault-name myVault \
  --policy-name DefaultPolicy \
  --resource-group myRG
```

Use the Azure Portal to configure alerting, notification, and test restores.

Testing and Automation of Failover/Backup

Disaster recovery isn't real unless it's tested.

Test Failover with Azure Site Recovery

- Allows you to replicate production VMs and perform non-disruptive tests.

```
az backup recoverypoint list \
  --vault-name myVault \
  --resource-group myRG \
  --item-name myVM
```

Trigger a **test failover** into a sandboxed network for validation.

Automate DR Testing with Azure Automation

Runbooks can test failover or backup integrity monthly:

```
# PowerShell snippet in Azure Automation
Start-AzRecoveryServicesBackupTestRestore \
  -ResourceGroupName myRG \
  -VaultName myVault \
  -ItemName myVM \
  -RestorePointId <id>
```

Send results to Log Analytics and alert on anomalies.

Patterns for Failover and Backup Architecture

Active-Passive (Warm Standby)

- Services run in a primary region.
- Secondary region is up but scaled down.
- On failure, scale up secondary and reroute traffic.

Pros:

- Cost-effective

- Reasonably fast RTO/RPO

Cons:

- Higher complexity
- Slightly longer failover time

Active-Active

- Services fully active in two or more regions.
- Front Door or Traffic Manager routes traffic to the closest or fastest endpoint.

Pros:

- Fastest failover
- High availability

Cons:

- Higher cost
- More complexity in data consistency

Backup-Only (Cold Standby)

- Services run in a single region.
- Backups stored in a secondary region.

Pros:

- Lowest cost

Cons:

- Longest RTO/RPO
- Manual provisioning needed

Choose based on business impact analysis and criticality.

Compliance, Governance, and Cost Control

Compliance

- Use Azure Policy to enforce backup configuration:
  - Ensure VMs are registered with Recovery Vaults.
  - Require GRS for critical workloads.

Governance

- Tag resources with recovery and SLA metadata.
- Use Azure Blueprints to enforce DR policies at scale.
- Store runbooks and DR documentation in shared wikis or repositories.

Cost

- Optimize storage tiers for long-term backup (e.g., Archive tier).
- Use deduplication and compression.
- Clean up unused backup data with retention policies.

Track costs using:

```
az consumption usage list --start-date 2024-01-01 --end-date 2024-01-31
```

Conclusion

Failover and backup are not optional in modern cloud architecture—they're essential. Azure provides a broad set of services to help architects design systems that **recover gracefully**, **retain data securely**, and **resume operations quickly** under stress.

By planning around RTO/RPO goals, automating failover, testing regularly, and aligning with organizational policies, you create systems that are not only resilient but trustworthy.

Combining **active monitoring**, **geo-redundancy**, and **versioned backups** ensures that your architecture supports not just availability—but continuity.

In the next chapter, we'll shift focus to **security** and explore how to design systems that are secure by default, enforcing identity, network, and data protection at every layer of your Azure infrastructure.

Chapter 5: Security by Design in Azure

Identity and Access Management (IAM)

Identity and Access Management (IAM) is the cornerstone of securing cloud infrastructure. In Azure, IAM governs **who** has access to **what**, and **how** that access is granted, controlled, and monitored. Unlike traditional networks secured by perimeter-based firewalls, cloud-native security emphasizes identity as the first line of defense—referred to as the **Zero Trust** model.

This section delves into Azure's IAM framework, which includes Azure Active Directory (Azure AD), role-based access control (RBAC), conditional access, managed identities, and governance tools such as policies and blueprints. These features work together to protect data, services, and resources from unauthorized access and internal threats.

Core Principles of Identity and Access Management

Azure IAM follows these guiding principles:

- **Least Privilege Access**: Grant users the minimum set of permissions required.

- **Separation of Duties**: Avoid assigning multiple high-privilege roles to the same user.

- **Just-in-Time Access**: Limit time-bound administrative access.

- **Auditing and Monitoring**: Continuously track who accessed what and when.

- **Policy Enforcement**: Automate security and compliance rules.

By adhering to these principles, architects can reduce risk while maintaining operational agility.

Azure Active Directory (Azure AD)

Azure AD is the identity provider for Microsoft cloud services. It supports:

- Authentication for users, devices, and applications

- Single Sign-On (SSO) across Azure, Microsoft 365, and SaaS apps

- Multi-Factor Authentication (MFA)

- Federation with on-prem Active Directory

- Conditional Access Policies

Azure AD is integrated with virtually every Azure resource, making it a foundation for secure identity management.

User Authentication and MFA

Enable MFA for all users, especially those with elevated privileges:

```
az ad user update --id user@domain.com --force-change-password-next-login true
```

In the Azure Portal:

- Navigate to **Azure AD** > **Security** > **MFA**
- Enforce MFA per user or via Conditional Access

Conditional Access

Conditional Access policies restrict access based on:

- User group or role
- Location/IP address
- Device state (compliant or not)
- Application sensitivity
- Sign-in risk

Example use case: Block access from outside your corporate IP range.

```
New-AzureADMSConditionalAccessPolicy `
  -DisplayName "Block External Access" `
  -Conditions @{ SignInRiskLevels = @("high"); Locations = @("AllTrusted") } `
  -GrantControls @{ BuiltInControls = @("block") }
```

These rules ensure only the right users, on the right devices, under the right conditions can access your resources.

Role-Based Access Control (RBAC)

Azure RBAC allows fine-grained access management for Azure resources. It enables you to:

- Assign roles to users, groups, or service principals

- Scope access to a subscription, resource group, or individual resource

- Use built-in roles or define custom roles

Built-in Roles

Role	Description
Owner	Full control including access management
Contributor	Full control except access management
Reader	View-only access
User Access Administrator	Manage user access without managing resources

To assign a role using CLI:

```
az role assignment create \
  --assignee user@domain.com \
  --role Contributor \
  --scope /subscriptions/<sub-id>/resourceGroups/myResourceGroup
```

Custom Roles

Define your own roles when built-in roles don't meet your requirements:

```
{

  "Name": "VM Start Stop Operator",

  "Actions": [

    "Microsoft.Compute/virtualMachines/start/action",

    "Microsoft.Compute/virtualMachines/deallocate/action"

  ],

  "AssignableScopes": ["/subscriptions/<sub-id>"]

}
```

RBAC is enforced in real-time and is fully auditable via Azure Activity Logs.

Managed Identities

Azure provides **Managed Identities** for applications running in Azure to securely access other Azure resources without storing credentials.

Types of Managed Identities

- **System-assigned**: Tied to a single resource (e.g., VM, Function App)

- **User-assigned**: Standalone identity reusable across multiple resources

Use case: A Function App writing to Azure Key Vault without a secret.

```
az identity create --name myIdentity --resource-group myRG


az functionapp identity assign \

  --name myFunctionApp \

  --resource-group myRG \

  --identities myIdentity
```

Grant the identity permissions in Key Vault:

```
az keyvault set-policy \
  --name myKeyVault \
  --object-id <identity-object-id> \
  --secret-permissions get list
```

No credentials are exposed, and rotation is handled automatically by Azure.

Azure AD Privileged Identity Management (PIM)

Privileged Identity Management (PIM) helps control and monitor access to privileged roles.

Key Features:

- Just-In-Time (JIT) access
- Approval workflows for role elevation
- Time-bound assignments
- Alerting and access reviews

Example: Configure JIT access for Subscription Contributor

```
az role assignment create \
  --role Contributor \
  --assignee <userPrincipalName> \
  --scope /subscriptions/<sub-id> \
  --condition-version 2.0 \
  --condition "user.accessLevel = 'Eligible'"
```

Use PIM to drastically reduce the attack surface of always-on privileged accounts.

Identity Governance and Compliance

Ensure access is governed, traceable, and compliant:

Access Reviews

Automate periodic reviews of group memberships, role assignments, and app access.

- Navigate to **Azure AD > Identity Governance > Access Reviews**
- Create recurring reviews for sensitive roles

Entitlement Management

Package permissions, roles, and access requests into **Access Packages** for onboarding/offboarding users.

- Useful for guest user management and B2B scenarios
- Supports approval workflows and expiration

Integration with Applications

Azure AD supports authentication protocols:

- **OAuth 2.0, OpenID Connect** for modern apps
- **SAML 2.0** for enterprise apps
- **WS-Fed** for legacy compatibility

Example: Registering an App

```
az ad app create \
  --display-name "MyApp" \
  --identifier-uris "https://myapp.contoso.com" \
  --reply-urls "https://myapp.contoso.com/auth"
```

Generate a service principal:

```
az ad sp create --id <app-id>
```

Applications can use **MSAL (Microsoft Authentication Library)** to authenticate users and acquire tokens for APIs.

Monitoring and Auditing Identity Access

Use **Azure Monitor**, **Log Analytics**, and **Microsoft Defender for Identity** to track anomalies.

Sample KQL Query: Admin Role Assignments

```
AuditLogs

| where OperationName == "Add member to role"

| where TargetResources contains "Owner"

| project TimeGenerated, InitiatedBy, TargetResources
```

Alerts and Notifications

- Enable alert rules for suspicious sign-ins or new global admin role assignments.

- Integrate with Sentinel or SIEM for enterprise-level analytics.

Best Practices

- Enforce **MFA** for all users.

- Apply **RBAC** with the narrowest possible scope.

- Use **managed identities** to eliminate credential exposure.

- Implement **PIM** for all privileged roles.

- Conduct regular **access** **reviews**.

- Monitor sign-ins and role changes continuously.

- Avoid using service principals with long-lived secrets.

- Integrate **Conditional** **Access** for Zero Trust enforcement.

- Document IAM policies and onboard developers/admins through access packages.

Conclusion

Securing identity and access in Azure is not merely about controlling who can log in—it's about building an intelligent, auditable, and adaptive security framework that aligns with modern threats and operational requirements. Azure's IAM ecosystem provides the tools needed to implement Zero Trust security by design.

By leveraging Azure AD, RBAC, PIM, and Conditional Access in harmony, architects can create secure-by-default environments that scale with the organization and resist modern attack vectors. In the next section, we will examine how to further secure your Azure environment using Defender for Cloud and Security Center to monitor, protect, and respond to threats in real-time.

Azure Security Center and Defender for Cloud

Securing cloud workloads is a dynamic challenge. As environments scale, so do the risks— from misconfigurations and vulnerabilities to malicious insiders and external threats. Azure offers **Microsoft Defender for Cloud** (formerly known as Azure Security Center) as a comprehensive solution for **security posture management** and **threat protection** across Azure, hybrid, and multi-cloud environments.

This section provides a deep dive into Defender for Cloud's capabilities, how to implement it effectively, how it integrates with compliance and governance models, and the key configurations needed to build a proactive, threat-aware architecture in Azure.

What Is Microsoft Defender for Cloud?

Microsoft Defender for Cloud is a **Cloud-Native Application Protection Platform (CNAPP)** that provides:

- **Security posture management**: Continuous assessment of Azure resources and recommendations to improve security.

- **Cloud workload protection**: Threat detection and response for VMs, containers, databases, and other workloads.

- **Defender plans**: Add-on protections for specific resources (e.g., Defender for App Services, Defender for SQL).

- **Multi-cloud support**: Integrates with AWS and GCP via connectors.

Key Capabilities

- Secure Score: Visual measure of your environment's overall security health

- Regulatory compliance dashboard

- Built-in hardening recommendations

- Real-time threat detection and alerts

- Security alerts triaged by severity

- Integration with Microsoft Sentinel, Logic Apps, and automation workflows

---

Enabling Defender for Cloud

Defender for Cloud is enabled by default at the subscription level, but **Defender plans** must be explicitly enabled for workload protection.

Enable via Azure Portal

1. Navigate to **Microsoft Defender for Cloud**.

2. Select **Environment Settings > Your Subscription**.

3. Enable relevant Defender plans:

   o Servers

   o Storage

   o SQL

   o Containers

   o App   Services o   Key   Vault

Enable via CLI

```
az security pricing create \

  --name VirtualMachines \

  --tier Standard \

  --resource-type Microsoft.Compute
```

Repeat for other resource types as needed (e.g., AppServices, SqlServers, KubernetesService).

Understanding Secure Score

Secure Score is a numeric value (0–100%) that reflects how well your environment aligns with Azure's security best practices. It is calculated based on:

- Resource   health

- Remediation   of   security   recommendations

- Coverage   of   Defender   plans

Each recommendation has an impact percentage, and completing it increases your overall Secure Score.

Improve Secure Score By:

- Enabling   just-in-time   (JIT)   VM   access

- Enforcing   MFA   on   all   user   accounts

- Remediating   exposed   ports   (e.g.,   3389,   22)

- Enabling   disk   encryption   for   VMs

- Applying   NSGs   and   ASGs   to   network   interfaces

Monitor and track changes via the Secure Score dashboard or API.

Recommendations and Hardening

Defender for Cloud continuously scans your resources and provides **security recommendations**, each tied to industry benchmarks such as:

- Azure   Security   Benchmark

- NIST   SP   800-53

- CIS   Controls

- ISO   27001

Example Recommendations:

- "Restrict   access   to   management   ports   on   your   VM"

- "Enable   advanced   data   security   for   SQL   Servers"

- "Deploy   Endpoint   Protection   on   virtual   machines"

- "Enable   vulnerability   assessment   for   your   App   Services"

Each recommendation includes remediation guidance and automation options.

Remediation via CLI

```
az security task list --query "[?state=='Active']"
```

Manually apply recommendations or use **autofix policies** with Azure Policy to enforce configurations at scale.

Threat Protection and Alerts

Defender for Cloud uses advanced analytics, threat intelligence, and behavioral heuristics to detect threats across your resources. When a threat is detected, it raises **security alerts**.

Example Alerts

- Brute-force   attacks   on   SSH/RDP   ports

- SQL injection attempts on web apps
- Suspicious process execution on VMs
- Credential harvesting in containers
- Data exfiltration via Storage Blob access

Each alert contains:

- Severity level (Low, Medium, High)
- Affected resources
- Mitigation steps
- Investigation guidance
- Integration path with SIEM or SOAR tools

Alerts can trigger Logic Apps for automated responses.

Just-In-Time VM Access (JIT)

JIT access allows you to reduce the attack surface by blocking all inbound traffic to management ports (e.g., 22, 3389) unless explicitly approved for a short window.

Enable JIT via CLI

```
az security jit-policy create \
  --name myVM \
  --resource-group myRG \
  --location eastus \
  --virtual-machines                        id=/subscriptions/<sub-id>/resourceGroups/myRG/providers/Microsoft.Compute/virtualMachines/myVM \
  --ports number=22 protocol=TCP allowedSourceAddressPrefix=1.2.3.4 maxRequestAccessDuration=PT1H
```

Access must be requested through Azure Portal or API, approved for a specific IP, port, and time window.

Integration with Azure Policy

Defender for Cloud recommendations are tightly integrated with **Azure Policy**. You can:

- Monitor compliance

- Assign policies to enforce baseline configurations

- Remediate non-compliance automatically

Example Policy Assignments

- "Audit VMs that do not have backup configured"

- "Deny untagged resources"

- "Deploy vulnerability scanner extensions automatically"

```
az policy assignment create \
  --name "EnforceMonitoring" \
  --scope /subscriptions/<sub-id> \
  --policy
"/providers/Microsoft.Authorization/policyDefinitions/audit-vm-extension"
```

Use **initiative definitions** to group multiple policies under a single compliance standard.

Regulatory Compliance and Benchmarks

Defender for Cloud includes a **regulatory compliance dashboard** that maps your environment to standards like:

- NIST

- HIPAA

- PCI   DSS

- ISO   27001

- Azure   Security   Benchmark

Each control shows your compliance status based on underlying recommendations and configurations.

Use compliance views to:

- Track   progress   toward   certification

- Identify   high-risk   non-compliant   resources

- Export   evidence   for   audits

Defender for Cloud in Hybrid and Multi-Cloud

Azure Arc Integration

Use **Azure Arc** to bring on-premises and multi-cloud resources under Defender's management:

- VMs   (Linux/Windows)   in   AWS,   GCP,   on-prem

- Kubernetes   clusters

- SQL   Servers

```
az connectedmachine onboarding create \

  --resource-group myRG \

  --machine-name myHybridVM \

  --location eastus
```

Defender extends its coverage beyond Azure-native services.

Automation and Incident Response

Integrate Defender for Cloud with **Azure Logic Apps** to automate response workflows:

- Isolate VMs on alert

- Rotate keys in Key Vault

- Notify SecOps via Teams or email

- Trigger remediation scripts

Example: Respond to High-Severity Alert

```
if (alert.Severity == "High") {

  Start-AzVM -Name "isolate-vm.ps1"

}
```

These automations enable real-time, repeatable, and traceable incident responses.

Pricing and Licensing

Defender for Cloud offers:

- **Free tier**: Posture management, secure score, recommendations

- **Defender plans**: Per-resource pricing model (e.g., per VM, per SQL DB)

Pricing examples (subject to change):

- $15/VM/month for Defender for Servers

- $7/SQL Server/month for Defender for SQL

Use the **Azure Pricing Calculator** and **Cost Management** dashboards to model and monitor costs.

Best Practices

- Enable Defender plans for all critical workloads.
- Monitor and regularly review Secure Score.
- Remediate top-priority recommendations first.
- Enable JIT VM access to reduce management exposure.
- Integrate alerts with Microsoft Sentinel or third-party SIEMs.
- Use Policy initiatives to standardize security baselines.
- Run periodic compliance audits using dashboards.
- Train DevOps teams to review Defender alerts during deployments.

Conclusion

Microsoft Defender for Cloud is a robust, intelligent, and extensible platform that turns reactive security into a proactive discipline. It enables architects and security teams to continuously monitor posture, respond to threats in real time, and ensure compliance at cloud speed and scale.

By incorporating Defender for Cloud into your architecture from the ground up, you don't just protect your workloads—you empower your teams to **detect, defend, and evolve** with the ever-changing threat landscape.

In the next section, we'll explore how to secure the network layer using Network Security Groups, Application Security Groups, and Azure-native firewalls to enforce perimeter and micro-segmentation strategies across your cloud environments.

Secure Networking: NSGs, ASGs, and Firewalls

As cloud environments grow in complexity, securing the network becomes a crucial pillar of any cloud security strategy. In Azure, network security is enforced through a combination of platform-native tools and services that help organizations apply **defense in depth**, **zero trust principles**, and **micro-segmentation**.

This section explores Azure's core network security mechanisms: **Network Security Groups (NSGs)**, **Application Security Groups (ASGs)**, and **Azure Firewall**. Together, these tools provide granular traffic control, visibility, and policy enforcement across your virtual networks.

Principles of Network Security in Azure

Effective network security in Azure is built on several foundational principles:

- **Least privilege**: Allow only required traffic and deny all else by default.

- **Segmentation**: Isolate workloads based on business logic, sensitivity, and communication requirements.

- **Layered defense**: Use NSGs for basic filtering, ASGs for application-layer groupings, and firewalls for advanced threat protection.

- **Logging and monitoring**: Capture logs and flow data to detect anomalies.

- **Zero Trust**: Trust nothing, verify everything—regardless of source or destination.

These principles are implemented through Azure's virtual network security capabilities.

Network Security Groups (NSGs)

A **Network Security Group (NSG)** is a stateful packet filter that controls inbound and outbound traffic to Azure resources within a virtual network. NSGs work at Layer 3 and Layer 4 of the OSI model.

NSG Components

- **Security Rules**: Define traffic filtering logic based on:

  - Source/destination IP

  - Source/destination port

  - Protocol (TCP/UDP)

  - Direction (inbound/outbound)

  - Priority (100–4096)

  - Action (Allow/Deny)

- **Default Rules**: Azure applies system-defined rules such as:

  - Allow VNet inbound

- ○ Allow Azure Load Balancer inbound
- ○ Deny all inbound by default

Applying NSGs

- To **subnets**: Controls traffic to all resources in the subnet.
- To **network interfaces**: Controls traffic to/from individual VMs.

Example: Creating and Assigning an NSG

```
az network nsg create \
  --resource-group myResourceGroup \
  --name myNSG


az network nsg rule create \
  --resource-group myResourceGroup \
  --nsg-name myNSG \
  --name AllowHTTP \
  --protocol Tcp \
  --direction Inbound \
  --priority 100 \
  --source-address-prefix Internet \
  --source-port-range '*' \
  --destination-address-prefix '*' \
  --destination-port-range 80 \
  --access Allow


az network vnet subnet update \
```

```
--resource-group myResourceGroup \

--vnet-name myVNet \

--name mySubnet \

--network-security-group myNSG
```

This NSG allows HTTP traffic from the internet to your subnet.

NSG Best Practices

- Always follow **deny-by-default**: Only allow necessary ports and IPs.

- Avoid opening RDP (3389) or SSH (22) to the internet—use JIT access instead.

- Use **tags** (e.g., `Internet`, `VirtualNetwork`, `AzureLoadBalancer`) for flexible rule management.

- Monitor NSG flow logs for unexpected patterns.

Application Security Groups (ASGs)

Application Security Groups (ASGs) simplify NSG rule management by grouping virtual machines based on **logical workloads** instead of IP addresses.

Benefits

- Manage access control for large, dynamic environments

- Eliminate hardcoding of IPs in NSG rules

- Enable micro-segmentation without IP constraints

Example: Creating and Using an ASG

```
az network asg create \

  --resource-group myResourceGroup \

  --name WebServersASG \

  --location eastus
```

```
az network nic update \

  --resource-group myResourceGroup \

  --name myVMNic \

  --application-security-groups WebServersASG
```

Then create an NSG rule referencing the ASG:

```
az network nsg rule create \

  --resource-group myResourceGroup \

  --nsg-name myNSG \

  --name AllowAppToDB \

  --direction Inbound \

  --priority 200 \

  --access Allow \

  --protocol Tcp \

  --source-asgs WebServersASG \

  --destination-address-prefix 10.0.2.0/24 \

  --destination-port-range 1433
```

This rule allows traffic from the Web ASG to a database subnet on port 1433.

ASG Best Practices

- Group VMs based on application role (e.g., Web, API, DB)
- Use with naming conventions for easier maintenance
- Combine with tagging for automation workflows

- Use ASGs in NSG rules to implement **service-tier firewalls**

Azure Firewall

Azure Firewall is a fully stateful, cloud-native network security appliance that provides advanced traffic filtering for your Azure Virtual Network. It supports both **east-west** (internal) and **north-south** (internet-facing) traffic control.

Key Features

- L3–L7 filtering (network, application, FQDN, TLS inspection)
- Threat intelligence integration
- DNS proxy and filtering
- SNAT for outbound connections
- Integration with Azure Monitor and Log Analytics
- Availability Zones for HA deployments

Azure Firewall SKUs

- **Standard**: Core functionality with threat detection.
- **Premium**: Adds TLS inspection, IDPS, URL filtering, and more granular policies.

Deploying Azure Firewall

To deploy Azure Firewall, you need a dedicated subnet called `AzureFirewallSubnet` and a public IP address.

```
az network vnet subnet create \

  --name AzureFirewallSubnet \

  --vnet-name myVNet \

  --resource-group myRG \

  --address-prefix 10.0.1.0/24
```

```
az network public-ip create \

  --name myFirewallPublicIP \

  --resource-group myRG \

  --sku Standard


az network firewall create \

  --name myFirewall \

  --resource-group myRG \

  --vnet-name myVNet \

  --public-ip-address myFirewallPublicIP
```

Create a Firewall Rule

```
az network firewall network-rule create \

  --firewall-name myFirewall \

  --resource-group myRG \

  --collection-name AllowDNS \

  --name AllowDNS \

  --rule-type NetworkRule \

  --priority 100 \

  --action Allow \

  --protocols UDP \

  --source-addresses '*' \

  --destination-addresses 168.63.129.16 \
```

```
--destination-ports 53
```

Use **route tables** to force traffic through the firewall by setting UDRs.

Advanced Security: Micro-Segmentation

Micro-segmentation is the practice of isolating workloads by their purpose and limiting traffic strictly to what's necessary. This is achievable in Azure using a combination of:

- **NSGs** to define per-subnet or per-VM security
- **ASGs** to define application groups
- **Azure Firewall** for L7 filtering and outbound inspection
- **Azure Policy** to enforce tag-based or port-based access control

Example: Block outbound access to storage services from non-app subnets:

```
{
  "if": {
    "allOf": [
      { "field": "type", "equals": "Microsoft.Network/networkSecurityGroups" },
      { "field": "Microsoft.Network/networkSecurityGroups/securityRules[*].destinationPortRange", "equals": "443" },
      { "field": "Microsoft.Network/networkSecurityGroups/securityRules[*].destinationAddressPrefix", "equals": "Storage" }
    ]
  },
  "then": {
    "effect": "deny"
```

```
  }

}
```

Monitoring and Logging

NSG Flow Logs

Enable NSG flow logs to capture traffic flow records for analysis and auditing.

```
az network watcher flow-log configure \

  --enabled true \

  --nsg myNSG \

  --resource-group myRG \

  --workspace myLogAnalyticsWorkspace \

  --retention 30
```

Flow logs are essential for detecting:

- Port   scans

- Unexpected   inbound   traffic

- Misconfigured   rules

Azure Firewall Logs

Firewall logs include:

- Application   rule   logs

- Network   rule   logs

- Threat   intelligence   alerts

Use **Kusto Query Language (KQL)** to analyze logs in Log Analytics:

```
AzureDiagnostics

| where ResourceType == "AZUREFIREWALLS"

| where OperationName == "AzureFirewallApplicationRuleLog"

| project TimeGenerated, msg_s, SourceIP_s, DestinationIP_s, Action_s
```

Best Practices

- Block all by default; explicitly allow only necessary traffic.

- Use **NSGs** at **subnet level** and **NIC level** for layered protection.

- Group resources into **ASGs** for logical policy enforcement.

- Use **Azure Firewall** for outbound control and L7 filtering.

- Monitor **flow logs and alerts** regularly.

- Use **Private Endpoints** and **Service Endpoints** to reduce public exposure.

- Apply **route tables** to steer traffic through inspection points.

- Define **tiered security zones** (e.g., public, DMZ, internal, restricted).

Conclusion

Network security in Azure is not a single service or setting—it's a layered, policy-driven system composed of NSGs, ASGs, firewalls, routing, and identity. Together, these elements form a comprehensive model for secure connectivity, segmentation, and traffic control.

By implementing a defense-in-depth strategy using NSGs and ASGs for micro-segmentation and Azure Firewall for advanced inspection and filtering, architects can enforce security at every boundary and ensure consistent governance across environments.

In the next section, we'll turn to data security and compliance—examining how Azure encrypts data in transit and at rest, and how to align your architecture with regulatory frameworks such as GDPR, HIPAA, and PCI DSS.

Data Encryption and Compliance Standards

Data security is at the heart of any cloud-based solution, particularly in regulated industries where sensitive information must be protected both technically and legally. Azure provides a rich set of tools and configurations to ensure **data confidentiality**, **integrity**, and **availability** through robust **encryption mechanisms** and **compliance controls**.

This section explores how Azure encrypts data at rest and in transit, manages keys, integrates with compliance standards like GDPR, HIPAA, ISO 27001, and PCI DSS, and offers the governance capabilities needed to audit, enforce, and maintain security over time.

The Importance of Encryption in Azure

Encryption transforms readable data into a cipher that can only be deciphered with the appropriate key. Azure applies encryption across all layers of the architecture, with mechanisms that support:

- **Default** **(platform-managed)** encryption

- **Customer-managed** keys **(CMK)**

- **Bring** **Your** **Own** **Key** **(BYOK)**

- **Double** **Encryption** for added assurance

- **End-to-end** **encryption** for in-transit data

These options empower customers to match their security controls to their threat models and regulatory requirements.

Encryption at Rest

All data stored in Azure is encrypted at rest by default using **256-bit AES encryption**, one of the strongest symmetric encryption algorithms available.

Key Scenarios for Encryption at Rest:

1. **Azure** **Storage** **Accounts** (Blob, Queue, Table, File)

2. **Azure** **SQL** **Database**

3. **Azure** **Managed** **Disks**

4. **Azure** **Cosmos** **DB**

5. **Azure**   **Backup**   **Vaults**

6. **Azure Key Vault** (for storing secrets, not for general-purpose storage)

Azure offers two models for key management:

- **Platform-managed keys (PMK)** – Azure manages the lifecycle of the encryption keys.

- **Customer-managed keys (CMK)** – You create and manage keys in Azure Key Vault.

Enabling Customer-Managed Keys for Azure Storage

1. Create   a   key   in   Azure   Key   Vault:

```
az keyvault key create \
  --vault-name myKeyVault \
  --name myCMK \
  --protection software
```

2. Assign   access   permissions:

```
az keyvault set-policy \
  --name myKeyVault \
  --object-id <storage-account-managed-identity> \
  --key-permissions wrapKey unwrapKey get
```

3. Associate   the   CMK   with   your   storage   account:

```
az storage account update \
  --name mystorageaccount \
```

```
--resource-group myResourceGroup \

--encryption-key-source Microsoft.Keyvault \

--encryption-key-vault myKeyVault \

--encryption-key-name myCMK
```

With CMKs, organizations retain control over key rotation, revocation, and auditing.

Double Encryption

For certain workloads, Azure supports **double encryption**—using two independent encryption layers for enhanced assurance. This is available on:

- Azure Storage accounts
- Azure Disk Encryption
- Azure SQL Managed Instance (in certain tiers)

When enabled, data is encrypted once at the application layer and again at the infrastructure layer.

Example: Combining **Transparent Data Encryption (TDE)** with **Storage Service Encryption (SSE)**.

Encryption in Transit

Encryption in transit ensures that data cannot be intercepted or tampered with as it moves between systems.

Mechanisms Include:

- **HTTPS/TLS 1.2+** – For all data movement over public endpoints
- **SMB 3.0 encryption** – For Azure Files
- **VPN/IPSec encryption** – For hybrid network connections
- **TLS for service-to-service traffic** – e.g., App Service → SQL DB

- **Private Endpoints** – For bypassing public internet entirely

Azure enforces TLS 1.2+ for most services and recommends disabling older, insecure protocols (TLS 1.0, 1.1) using custom configurations and policies.

Example: Enforce TLS 1.2 on an App Service:

```
az webapp update \
  --name myWebApp \
  --resource-group myResourceGroup \
  --https-only true \
  --min-tls-version 1.2
```

Azure Disk Encryption (ADE)

Azure Disk Encryption uses **BitLocker** (Windows) or **dm-crypt** (Linux) to encrypt OS and data disks attached to virtual machines.

Supports:

- Integration with Azure Key Vault (for CMKs)
- Encryption of both OS and data disks
- Auditing of key usage and access attempts

```
az vm encryption enable \
  --resource-group myResourceGroup \
  --name myVM \
  --disk-encryption-keyvault myKeyVault \
  --key-encryption-key myKey
```

ADE is particularly valuable for compliance with strict regulatory standards.

Azure Key Vault

Azure Key Vault is a secure key management service that supports:

- Secrets management (e.g., passwords, API keys)

- Key management (e.g., encryption keys for disks, databases)

- Certificate management (e.g., TLS/SSL)

- Hardware Security Module (HSM) backed keys

Key Vault Best Practices

- Enable **soft delete** and **purge protection**

- Use **access policies** or **RBAC** for permission control

- Monitor access via **Log Analytics**

- Automate **key rotation** every 90–180 days

Enable logging:

```
az monitor diagnostic-settings create \
  --name kv-logs \
  --resource                               /subscriptions/<sub-
id>/resourceGroups/myRG/providers/Microsoft.KeyVault/vaults/myKeyVau
lt \
  --workspace myLogAnalyticsWorkspace \
  --logs '[{"category":"AuditEvent","enabled":true}]'
```

Compliance in Azure

Azure meets a wide array of **global**, **regional**, and **industry-specific** compliance standards.

Global Standards

- **ISO/IEC** **27001**
- **SOC** 1, 2, **3**
- **CSA** **STAR**

Regional Standards

- **GDPR** (EU)
- **UK** **Cyber** **Essentials**
- **Australian** **IRAP**
- **Canada's** **PIPEDA**

Industry Standards

- **HIPAA/HITECH** – Healthcare
- **PCI** **DSS** – Payment card industry
- **FedRAMP** – U.S. government
- **CJIS** – Law enforcement

Azure provides **compliance reports and audit artifacts** via the **Service Trust Portal**.

Azure Policy for Encryption and Compliance

Azure Policy allows you to enforce and audit encryption standards across your environment.

Example: Policy to Ensure Storage Accounts Use CMK

```
{
  "if": {
    "allOf": [
      {
        "field": "type",
```

```
        "equals": "Microsoft.Storage/storageAccounts"

    },

    {

        "field":
"Microsoft.Storage/storageAccounts/encryption.keySource",

        "notequals": "Microsoft.Keyvault"

    }

  ]

},

"then": {

  "effect": "deny"

}

}
```

You can also use built-in policies like:

- "Audit unencrypted managed disks"
- "Enforce TLS 1.2 for App Services"
- "Deploy secure transfer required for storage accounts"

Assign these policies via the Azure Policy portal or CLI.

Governance and Auditing

Security controls mean little without **governance** and **auditability**. Azure provides:

- **Azure Monitor** for tracking security events
- **Azure Activity Logs** for changes and operations

- **Azure** **Defender** **for** **Cloud** integration
- **Microsoft** **Sentinel** for SIEM capabilities

Example: Track who accessed a Key Vault secret:

```
AzureDiagnostics
| where ResourceType == "VAULTS"
| where OperationName == "SecretGet"
| project TimeGenerated, CallerIpAddress, Identity, ResultType
```

Audit logs are essential for compliance reporting, forensic investigations, and trust assurance.

Encryption for Specific Azure Services

Service	Encryption Type	Key Control Options
Azure SQL DB	Transparent Data Encryption (TDE)	Platform or customer-managed keys
Azure Cosmos DB	Encryption at rest + transit	CMK supported
Azure Synapse	TDE + CMK	Enabled by default
Azure Blob Storage	SSE with AES-256	PMK or CMK + RBAC integration
Azure Kubernetes	Secret encryption via etcd	Custom plugins (in preview)

When possible, use **customer-managed keys** and **private endpoints** to maximize protection.

Best Practices

- Use **CMK** wherever possible for full control over key lifecycle.

- Store secrets in **Azure Key Vault**, not in code or environment variables.

- Enable **Secure Transfer Required** on all storage accounts.

- Enforce **TLS 1.2+** and **HTTPS-only** access across services.

- Implement **double encryption** for sensitive workloads.

- Use **Azure Policy** to audit and enforce encryption standards.

- Rotate encryption keys and secrets regularly.

- Enable **monitoring and alerting** for unauthorized access attempts.

Conclusion

Data encryption and regulatory compliance are non-negotiables in modern cloud architecture. Azure provides flexible, scalable, and powerful tools to secure your data at rest and in transit, while giving you control over key management and full visibility into access and usage.

By combining encryption with Azure's compliance certifications, policy engine, and monitoring tools, you can build trust with customers, satisfy auditors, and protect your business-critical information against threats—both internal and external.

In the next chapter, we'll look at how to design and deploy multi-tier and microservices-based applications on Azure, leveraging managed services and patterns that enhance agility, scalability, and maintainability across environments.

Chapter 6: Architecting Multi-Tier and Microservices Applications

Monolithic vs. Microservices Architectures

Designing applications that are scalable, maintainable, and resilient requires careful consideration of the application's architectural paradigm. Two predominant models dominate modern software architecture: **monolithic applications** and **microservices architectures**. While each has its place, choosing the right approach depends on your team's capabilities, system requirements, deployment goals, and future scalability needs.

This section explores the characteristics, benefits, trade-offs, and Azure-native services that support both monolithic and microservices designs. It also outlines migration strategies from monoliths to microservices and provides deployment guidance for each pattern using Azure tools and services.

Understanding Monolithic Architecture

A **monolithic application** is built as a single, unified codebase where all functionalities—UI, business logic, data access, and backend services—are tightly coupled and deployed together.

Characteristics

- Single deployment unit
- Tightly coupled components
- Centralized data store
- Common tech stack across all layers
- Typically hosted as a single web or API service

Advantages

- Simple to develop for small teams or MVPs
- Easier to deploy in early stages
- Straightforward debugging and tracing

- Lower initial complexity

Disadvantages

- Hard to scale parts independently

- Tight coupling makes changes risky

- Longer build and deploy times

- Difficult to adopt new tech incrementally

- Poor fault isolation—one bug can bring down the entire system

---

Understanding Microservices Architecture

A **microservices architecture** breaks the application into smaller, independent services. Each service is responsible for a specific function (e.g., user management, billing, inventory) and communicates with others through APIs or messaging systems.

Characteristics

- Services are independently deployable

- Each service has its own database (polyglot persistence)

- Services can use different languages or frameworks

- Decentralized development and ownership

- Communication over HTTP/REST, gRPC, or message brokers

Advantages

- Scalability of individual components

- Faster, safer deployments (CI/CD pipelines per service)

- Improved resilience and fault isolation

- Greater flexibility in tech stack choices

- Easier team autonomy and parallel development

Disadvantages

- Operational complexity (observability, testing, deployment)
- Requires mature DevOps and CI/CD practices
- Distributed system challenges (e.g., latency, eventual consistency)
- Requires careful API and service contract design

When to Use Monolith vs. Microservices

Factor	Monolithic	Microservices
Team size	Small	Medium to large
Initial product maturity	Early-stage, MVP	Mature, scalable
Deployment frequency	Infrequent	Frequent and independent
Fault isolation	Low	High
Scaling needs	Uniform scaling	Independent service scaling
Tech stack uniformity	Same for all components	Can vary per service
Operational overhead	Lower	Higher

For many applications, a **modular monolith** (well-structured, single-deployable app) is an excellent starting point. You can gradually refactor into microservices as the system grows.

Azure Services for Monolithic Applications

Azure supports monolithic workloads through multiple hosting options:

Azure App Service

- Ideal for hosting web apps or APIs
- Supports .NET, Node.js, Python, Java, PHP
- Built-in autoscaling and deployment slots

```
az webapp create \
  --resource-group myRG \
  --plan myAppServicePlan \
  --name myWebApp \
  --runtime "DOTNET|6.0"
```

Azure Virtual Machines

- Full control over OS and runtime
- Supports custom software and legacy apps
- Use Availability Sets or Zones for HA

Azure SQL Database

- Centralized relational data store
- Supports TDE and Active Geo-Replication
- Excellent for stateful monoliths

Azure Services for Microservices Applications

Microservices benefit from distributed services and serverless integration. Azure provides a robust ecosystem:

Azure Kubernetes Service (AKS)

- Fully managed Kubernetes
- Ideal for containerized microservices
- Supports horizontal scaling, service discovery, and ingress

```
az aks create \
  --resource-group myRG \
  --name myAKSCluster \
  --node-count 3 \
  --enable-addons monitoring \
  --generate-ssh-keys
```

Deploy microservices using Helm charts, YAML, or GitOps pipelines.

Azure Container Apps

- Simplified container orchestration for microservices
- Supports scale-to-zero and Dapr integration
- Built-in service-to-service communication

```
az containerapp create \
  --name myApp \
  --resource-group myRG \
  --image myregistry.azurecr.io/myapp:v1 \
  --environment myEnv
```

Azure Functions

- Best for event-driven, stateless microservices

- Auto-scales per event
- Supports multiple languages and bindings

```
func init MyFunctionApp --worker-runtime dotnet
func new --name ProcessOrder --template "HTTP trigger"
```

Azure Cosmos DB

- Globally distributed, multi-model database
- Perfect for decentralized, scalable microservices
- Supports per-service data ownership

Azure Service Bus / Event Grid

- Enables asynchronous communication between services
- Ensures decoupling and resilience
- Supports queues, topics, events, and pub/sub

Migrating from Monolith to Microservices

Migrating is rarely an overnight change. A phased approach is best:

Step 1: Identify Domains

- Use **Domain-Driven Design (DDD)** to break application into business domains.
- Create bounded contexts for potential services.

Step 2: Decouple the Data

- Avoid tightly coupled schemas.
- Extract data per service gradually (use database views or replication for interim stages).

Step 3: Introduce APIs or Messaging

- Create API layers to expose service contracts.

- Use asynchronous messaging for loosely coupled interactions.

Step 4: Containerize and Deploy Services

- Use Docker for packaging

- Deploy to AKS or Azure Container Apps

- Implement health checks, logging, and monitoring

Step 5: Build CI/CD Pipelines

- Create separate pipelines for each service.

- Implement automated testing and canary deployments.

Monitoring and Observability

Microservices demand enhanced observability due to their distributed nature.

Azure Tools

- **Application Insights**: End-to-end tracing, performance metrics

- **Log Analytics**: Query and analyze logs across services

- **Azure Monitor**: Metrics and alerts for resources

- **Azure Dapr** (Distributed Application Runtime): Built-in observability for microservices

Kusto Query Example (Application Insights):

```
requests
| where timestamp > ago(1h)
| summarize avg(duration) by name
```

Security in Microservices

Each service must be secured individually:

- Use **Azure Key Vault** to store secrets
- Implement **API gateways** with authentication
- Use **managed identities** to access Azure services
- Apply **network security** via NSGs and private endpoints
- Enforce **Zero Trust** principles

Best Practices

- **Design for failure**: Retry policies, circuit breakers, bulkheads
- **Use versioned APIs** to manage changes without breaking consumers
- **Centralize logging and tracing**
- **Define clear service ownership** across teams
- **Keep services small but meaningful**—not every function needs to be its own service
- **Use service mesh (e.g., Istio, Linkerd)** if you require fine-grained traffic control and policy enforcement

Conclusion

Choosing between a monolithic or microservices architecture is not just a technical decision—it's a strategic one. Monoliths offer simplicity and speed in early stages, while microservices provide the flexibility, scalability, and resilience needed for complex and evolving systems.

Azure provides a rich set of tools to support both paradigms. With services like App Service and Azure SQL for monoliths, and AKS, Container Apps, Cosmos DB, and Event Grid for microservices, architects can evolve their applications without abandoning past investments.

In the next section, we'll explore how to expose, manage, and secure APIs across these architectures using Azure's API Management and Gateway services.

API Management and Gateway Services

APIs (Application Programming Interfaces) are the connective tissue of modern applications. They enable services to communicate, expose business capabilities, and empower both internal and external consumers to interact with systems efficiently. As application architectures evolve into distributed systems and microservices, managing APIs becomes increasingly complex and critical to the success of the architecture.

This section explores Azure's approach to API management and gateway functionality, focusing on **Azure API Management (APIM)**, **Azure Application Gateway**, and **Azure Functions Proxies**. We'll dive into deployment models, design patterns, security, versioning, and observability—offering practical guidance for building resilient and scalable API ecosystems.

The Role of API Management in Cloud Architectures

In a microservices or multi-tiered environment, managing APIs is about more than just routing traffic. You need to:

- Secure and authenticate traffic

- Throttle and rate-limit requests

- Analyze usage and performance

- Transform and aggregate responses

- Enforce policies across services

- Monitor and debug service interactions

Azure API Management is a fully managed service designed to help you address these challenges while exposing your services internally, to partners, or to the public.

Azure API Management (APIM)

Azure API Management acts as a **gateway** between clients and your backend services. It provides a central point to manage, publish, secure, and monitor APIs across all environments.

Core Components

- **API Gateway**: Handles requests, forwards them to the correct backend, and applies policies.

- **Developer Portal**: Customizable web UI for developers to explore APIs and retrieve keys.

- **Publisher Portal (Azure Portal)**: Admin interface for API definition, security, and monitoring.

- **Management Plane**: REST APIs and Azure CLI for automation.

API Management Tiers

Tier	Description
Developer	For testing, development, and proof of concept
Basic	Entry-level production use, no SLA
Standard	Production-ready with SLA and autoscaling
Premium	Multi-region, VNet support, higher throughput
Consumption	Serverless pay-per-call API gateway (preview/GA)

Use **Premium** tier for global-scale, multi-region deployments. Use **Consumption** for lightweight use cases.

Creating an API Management Instance

```
az apim create \
  --name myAPIM \
  --resource-group myRG \
  --location eastus \
  --publisher-email admin@example.com \
```

```
--publisher-name "MyCompany"
```

Import APIs using OpenAPI, WSDL, or manually define them in the portal.

```
az apim api import \

  --resource-group myRG \

  --service-name myAPIM \

  --path myapi \

  --api-id myapiid \

  --specification-format OpenApi \

  --specification-path ./openapi.json
```

Defining and Publishing APIs

You can group APIs by products (e.g., internal, partner, public) and apply different policies per product.

Common Policies

- **Rate limiting**: Limit requests per user/IP.

- **JWT validation**: Validate incoming tokens.

- **IP filtering**: Allow/block based on IP.

- **Request transformation**: Modify headers, bodies, or URLs.

- **Caching**: Store responses for high-performance reads.

Example policy: Limit to 10 requests per minute

```
<rate-limit calls="10" renewal-period="60" />
```

Example policy: JWT validation

```
<validate-jwt    header-name="Authorization"    failed-validation-
httpcode="401" require-scheme="Bearer">

    <openid-config    url="https://login.microsoftonline.com/<tenant-
id>/v2.0/.well-known/openid-configuration" />

    <required-claims>

        <claim name="aud">

            <value>api://myapiid</value>

        </claim>

    </required-claims>

</validate-jwt>
```

API Versioning and Revisioning

Versioning is critical for backward compatibility and phased deployments. APIM supports:

- **URL path-based versioning**: `/v1/users, /v2/users`

- **Query string versioning**: `/users?api-version=1.0`

- **Header-based versioning**: `X-API-Version: 1.0`

Each version is managed independently, enabling A/B testing and safe rollout of new features.

Revisions are used for testing or staging changes before publishing them to a version.

Developer Experience and DevPortals

The **Developer Portal** allows developers to:

- Browse API documentation

- Test endpoints interactively

- Subscribe to products

- Retrieve API keys or tokens

You can customize the developer portal with your branding, navigation, and content. This is particularly useful for partner or external APIs.

Enable self-service onboarding and email confirmation to reduce friction for API consumers.

Securing APIs

Authentication Options

- **API Key**: Simple, shared secret model

- **OAuth 2.0**: For user-based access (interactive apps)

- **Client credentials flow**: For service-to-service communication

- **Azure AD B2C**: For consumer-facing APIs

- **Subscription keys**: Track usage and assign quotas

APIM can enforce all of the above using policies.

Backend Authentication

APIM can also inject authentication tokens to communicate securely with backend services (e.g., Azure Functions, App Services, or Logic Apps).

Use **Managed Identity** to securely connect to protected backend services:

```
az apim update \

  --name myAPIM \

  --resource-group myRG \

  --set identity.type="SystemAssigned"
```

Grant access in Azure Function or Key Vault using this identity.

Integration with Application Gateway

While APIM is an API gateway, **Azure Application Gateway** serves as a **web traffic load balancer with Layer 7 routing**. It can sit in front of APIM for enhanced features like:

- WAF (Web Application Firewall) protection

- URL-based routing

- SSL termination

- Custom error pages

Architecture:

```
Client → App Gateway (WAF) → API Management → Backend Services
```

This layered approach enables **centralized security**, **rate limiting**, and **insightful analytics** without exposing backend services.

Monitoring and Observability

Built-in Tools

- **Azure Monitor**: Resource-level metrics and alerts

- **Application Insights**: Telemetry, logs, request traces

- **Log Analytics**: Query logs across services

- **Diagnostic Logs**: Request/response logging

Example KQL Query: Latency by API operation

```
AzureDiagnostics

| where ResourceType == "APIManagementGatewayLogs"

| summarize avg(DurationMs) by OperationName_s
```

Set up alerts on:

- High   latency

- API   errors

- Unauthorized   access   attempts

- Quota   breaches

DevOps and Automation

Use ARM, Bicep, or Terraform to automate APIM deployment and configuration.

Example: Bicep for APIM

```
resource apiManagement 'Microsoft.ApiManagement/service@2021-08-01' =
{

  name: 'myAPIM'

  location: 'eastus'

  sku: {

    name: 'Consumption'

    capacity: 0

  }

  properties: {

    publisherEmail: 'admin@example.com'

    publisherName: 'MyCompany'

  }

}
```

Integrate APIM configurations into your CI/CD pipelines using **GitHub Actions**, **Azure DevOps**, or **APIM DevOps Toolkit**.

Best Practices

- Define **clear** **product** **boundaries** in APIs.

- Use **policies** to enforce rate limits, security, and transformation.

- Deploy a **developer** **portal** to accelerate onboarding.

- Choose **Premium** **tier** for global or enterprise-scale needs.

- Use **Consumption** **tier** for lightweight or serverless use cases.

- Implement **API** **lifecycle** **management** with versioning and revisions.

- Monitor usage and optimize underperforming endpoints.

- Use **WAF-enabled Application Gateway** in front of APIM for L7 protection.

- Use **Azure Private Link** to restrict backend communication to private networks.

Conclusion

API management is a central pillar of any modern cloud architecture. Whether you're building microservices, mobile backends, or partner integrations, Azure API Management provides a secure, scalable, and developer-friendly gateway for publishing, protecting, and monitoring your APIs.

With fine-grained control over traffic, policies, and observability, you can deliver APIs that are not just functional—but robust, consistent, and secure.

In the next section, we'll explore Azure's two major microservices platforms—Service Fabric and Azure Kubernetes Service—and how to choose between them when designing for scale, resiliency, and modularity.

Service Fabric vs. Azure Kubernetes Service

Designing and deploying microservices in a scalable, resilient, and manageable way requires the right orchestration platform. Azure offers two primary choices for containerized and microservices-based architectures: **Azure Service Fabric** and **Azure Kubernetes Service (AKS)**. While both are powerful platforms for deploying distributed applications, their models, tooling, and operating philosophies differ significantly.

This section provides an in-depth comparison of Service Fabric and AKS, including their architecture, capabilities, operational complexity, and the scenarios in which each is best suited. Understanding these differences is critical for making informed architectural decisions and aligning platform choice with organizational capabilities and goals.

Overview of Azure Service Fabric

Azure Service Fabric is a distributed systems platform developed by Microsoft. It's the underlying technology powering Azure core services such as Azure SQL Database, Azure Cosmos DB, and Event Hubs. It supports building and managing scalable and reliable microservices and containerized applications.

Key Features

- Support for stateful and stateless services
- Built-in service discovery and health monitoring
- Strong consistency guarantees for stateful services
- Rolling upgrades with automatic rollback
- Integration with .NET, Java, Windows, and Linux workloads
- Custom placement policies and application partitioning
- Direct programming model or guest executable/container support

Architecture

Service Fabric clusters are composed of nodes, which can be VMs or physical servers. Applications are deployed as services, which run on nodes and are managed by the Service Fabric runtime.

- **Cluster**: Logical grouping of nodes
- **Application**: A collection of services and configuration
- **Service**: The deployment unit, which can be stateless or stateful
- **Partition**: Divides service data and workload for scalability
- **Replica/Instance**: Multiple copies of services for redundancy

Service Fabric includes a **Reliable Services API** and **Reliable Actors framework**, offering a programming model for stateful services with automatic data replication and failover.

Overview of Azure Kubernetes Service (AKS)

Azure Kubernetes Service (AKS) is a managed Kubernetes platform. Kubernetes is the most widely adopted container orchestration system, designed for running stateless and stateful containerized applications at scale.

Key Features

- Fully managed control plane (master nodes)
- Native support for containers and Helm charts
- Horizontal Pod Autoscaling
- Node autoscaling and OS updates
- CI/CD pipeline integrations (GitHub Actions, Azure DevOps)
- RBAC and network policies
- Observability via Azure Monitor and Prometheus/Grafana
- Supports Windows and Linux containers

Architecture

Kubernetes is built around a declarative model, where you describe the desired state and the system ensures it is maintained.

- **Pods**: Basic deployment unit, can host one or more containers
- **Deployments**: Manage replicas of Pods, handle rolling updates
- **Services**: Expose Pods internally or externally
- **Ingress**: HTTP routing layer
- **StatefulSets**: Specialized resource for stateful services
- **Namespaces**: Isolate workloads within the same cluster

AKS abstracts away the complexities of managing the Kubernetes control plane while giving full control over worker nodes and deployments.

Comparing Service Fabric and AKS

Feature	Service Fabric	Azure Kubernetes Service (AKS)
Origin	Microsoft-built platform	CNCF (Cloud Native Computing Foundation)
Container Support	Docker containers, guest executables	Docker/OCI containers
State Management	Built-in for stateful services	StatefulSets, external storage, operators
Scaling	Manual or custom logic	HPA, Cluster Autoscaler
Service Discovery	Built-in	DNS-based, integrated
Upgrades	Rolling with rollback	Rolling deployments via Deployments
Programming Model	Native APIs (Reliable Services, Actors)	Kubernetes APIs (YAML, kubectl, CRDs)
Ecosystem Support	Limited external tooling	Rich ecosystem (Helm, Istio, Argo, etc.)
Multi-cloud	No	Yes (Kubernetes is vendor-neutral)
Community	Microsoft-driven	Global open-source community

When to Choose Azure Service Fabric

Service Fabric excels in scenarios requiring:

- **High availability with strong consistency** for stateful workloads
- **Complex orchestration of services with custom placement**
- **Low latency, high-throughput systems**
- **Tight integration with Windows/.NET applications**
- **Actor-based models** for high-scale simulations and IOT

Example Use Cases

- Financial systems that need replicated, consistent state
- Real-time multiplayer game servers
- Mission-critical applications with custom fault domains
- Migrated on-prem Service Fabric workloads

When to Choose Azure Kubernetes Service

AKS is often the better fit when:

- You require **container-first development**
- You want access to the **rich CNCF ecosystem**
- Your teams already use Docker and Kubernetes
- You need multi-cloud or hybrid deployment options
- You want **industry-standard tooling** (e.g., Helm, GitOps)

Example Use Cases

- Web and API services with microservices
- CI/CD-enabled DevOps environments

- Polyglot systems (e.g., Go, Python, Java, .NET)
- ML workloads and batch processing with autoscaling
- Startups or ISVs building cloud-native SaaS platforms

Operating Models

Service Fabric

Deployment via PowerShell, Azure CLI, or Visual Studio. Configuration requires manual definition of application and service manifests.

Example:

```
<ServiceManifest>

  <ServiceType>

    <StatelessServiceType ServiceTypeName="FrontendType" />

  </ServiceType>

</ServiceManifest>
```

Service Fabric Explorer offers UI-based management and visualization of services, health, and node status.

AKS

Deployment via Kubernetes manifests or Helm charts.

Example Deployment YAML:

```
apiVersion: apps/v1

kind: Deployment

metadata:

  name: myapp

spec:
```

```
replicas: 3

selector:

  matchLabels:

    app: myapp

template:

  metadata:

    labels:

      app: myapp

  spec:

    containers:

    - name: mycontainer

      image: myacr.azurecr.io/myimage:v1

      ports:

      - containerPort: 80
```

Use kubectl for managing workloads and Helm for packaging.

Observability and Monitoring

Service Fabric

- Native health reporting APIs
- Integration with Azure Monitor
- Visual diagnostics through Service Fabric Explorer
- Logging via EventSource, ETW, or Application Insights

AKS

- Prometheus and Grafana for custom metrics
- Azure Monitor and Container Insights for full cluster monitoring
- Fluent Bit and Log Analytics for logging
- Kubernetes events and metrics accessible via KQL queries

Example KQL:

```
KubePodInventory
| summarize count() by ClusterName, Namespace, ContainerID,
ContainerStatus
```

Developer Productivity and Ecosystem

Kubernetes enjoys a massive open-source community, which means:

- Faster innovation
- Third-party plugins (e.g., cert-manager, Open Policy Agent)
- Support for modern patterns like service mesh (Istio, Linkerd)
- Cloud-native build tools (Draft, Skaffold, Tilt)
- CI/CD with GitHub Actions, Argo CD, Flux

Service Fabric has a more opinionated programming model and smaller ecosystem but excels where deep integration and performance are paramount.

Security Models

Service Fabric

- Integrated with Azure AD for cluster authentication
- TLS encryption for node communication

- Role-based access for application packages

AKS

- Azure RBAC integration with Kubernetes RBAC
- Network policies for pod-level firewall rules
- Integration with Azure Key Vault for secrets
- Built-in container scanning with Defender for Containers

Migration Considerations

If moving from **Service Fabric to AKS**:

- Refactor stateful services to use external storage (e.g., Azure Cosmos DB, Redis)
- Break services into stateless APIs if possible
- Replace Reliable Services API with REST/gRPC endpoints
- Use Helm or Kustomize for deployment templates
- Evaluate Dapr as a runtime abstraction for distributed service patterns

If moving to **Service Fabric from traditional VMs or on-prem**, ensure your team is comfortable with the programming model and operational requirements.

Conclusion

Both Azure Service Fabric and Azure Kubernetes Service are robust platforms for running scalable, distributed applications. The choice depends on your team's expertise, architectural requirements, and ecosystem alignment.

- Choose **Service Fabric** for tight Windows/.NET integration, strong stateful service guarantees, and custom orchestration needs.
- Choose **AKS** for open-source flexibility, container-first workloads, community innovation, and a modern DevOps ecosystem.

In the next section, we'll explore how to build event-driven applications using **Azure Event Grid**, **Service Bus**, and **Event Hubs**—critical tools for enabling decoupled communication and real-time data processing in microservices architectures.

Event-Driven Architectures with Event Grid and Service Bus

Modern cloud-native applications are increasingly built around **event-driven architectures (EDA)**. This paradigm promotes responsiveness, scalability, decoupling, and flexibility by enabling components to communicate through the generation, detection, consumption, and reaction to events. In Azure, two cornerstone services support this model: **Azure Event Grid** and **Azure Service Bus**.

This section explores event-driven architectural principles, compares messaging options, and provides practical guidance for using Event Grid and Service Bus in scalable, loosely coupled systems. We'll cover event types, message delivery guarantees, routing patterns, architectural use cases, and integration with other Azure services.

What is Event-Driven Architecture?

An **event** is any significant change in state—for example, a file being uploaded to storage, a user registering on a website, or a sensor reading being emitted. In EDA, instead of services directly calling one another (tight coupling), they emit events that other services **subscribe** to and **react** upon.

Benefits of EDA:

- **Loose coupling**: Services don't need to know each other.

- **Asynchronous communication**: Enhances performance and scalability.

- **High extensibility**: New subscribers can be added without modifying publishers.

- **Resilience**: Failures in one part of the system don't cascade.

Key Concepts in Azure Messaging

Azure provides several services for EDA and messaging. The three most common are:

Service	Use Case	Protocol	Model

Event Grid	Lightweight, reactive eventing	HTTP	Push-publish-subscribe
Service Bus	Enterprise-grade message queue/topic	AMQP/HTTP	Brokered messaging
Event Hubs	High-throughput event ingestion (telemetry)	AMQP	Streaming

This section focuses on **Event Grid** and **Service Bus**, which are used for orchestrating and communicating between components in microservice and serverless architectures.

Azure Event Grid

Event Grid is a serverless, fully managed event routing service that uses the **publish-subscribe** model. It is optimized for high-speed, reactive scenarios where events are generated and subscribers respond in near real-time.

Key Features

- Push-based delivery via HTTP/HTTPS
- Near-instantaneous event propagation (< 100ms)
- Native integration with Azure services (e.g., Blob Storage, Resource Groups, Key Vault)
- Supports custom topics and event schemas
- Supports retry policies and dead-lettering
- High scalability and low latency

Event Sources

- Azure Blob Storage
- Azure Resource Manager

- Azure Maps
- Azure Media Services
- Azure Machine Learning
- IoT Hub
- Custom apps or services (via Custom Topics)

Event Handlers

- Azure Functions
- Azure Logic Apps
- Azure Event Hubs
- Azure Webhooks
- Azure Automation

Event Grid Example

Publish custom events to Event Grid:

1. Create a custom topic:

```
az eventgrid topic create \
  --name myTopic \
  --resource-group myRG \
  --location eastus
```

2. Publish an event:

```
az eventgrid event publish \
  --topic-name myTopic \
```

```
  --resource-group myRG \

  --event-file myevent.json
```

Example JSON event format:

```
[

  {

    "id": "1234",

    "eventType": "OrderCreated",

    "subject": "/orders/5678",

    "eventTime": "2025-04-21T10:00:00Z",

    "data": {

      "orderId": "5678",

      "total": 99.99

    },

    "dataVersion": "1.0"

  }

]
```

Subscription and Delivery

3. Create an event subscription to a handler:

```
az eventgrid event-subscription create \

  --name mySubscription \
```

```
  --source-resource-id                    "/subscriptions/<sub-
id>/resourceGroups/myRG/providers/Microsoft.EventGrid/topics/myTopic
" \

  --endpoint-type webhook \

  --endpoint https://myapp.azurewebsites.net/api/events
```

Event Grid will deliver events to the specified endpoint. Retries are automatically attempted on failure using exponential backoff.

Azure Service Bus

Azure Service Bus is an enterprise-grade message broker that supports **asynchronous message processing**, **ordered delivery**, **dead-lettering**, and **transactions**. It's ideal for scenarios requiring complex routing, guaranteed delivery, and high reliability.

Key Features

- Queues and topics/subscriptions
- FIFO message ordering
- Duplicate detection
- Scheduled delivery
- Dead-lettering
- Session-based messaging
- Batching and transactions

Queues vs. Topics

Feature	Queue	Topic/Subscribers
Model	Point-to-point	Publish-subscribe

Delivery	Single consumer	Multiple subscribers
Use Case	Decoupling producer and single worker	Fan-out messages to many consumers

Creating a Queue

```
az servicebus namespace create \

  --name myNamespace \

  --resource-group myRG \

  --location eastus \

  --sku Standard


az servicebus queue create \

  --name myQueue \

  --namespace-name myNamespace \

  --resource-group myRG
```

Send a message using the SDK or REST API.

Using Topics and Subscriptions

Topics allow you to publish a message once and deliver it to many subscribers, each with optional filters.

```
az servicebus topic create \

  --name myTopic \

  --namespace-name myNamespace \
```

```
    --resource-group myRG


az servicebus topic subscription create \

    --name mySubscription \

    --namespace-name myNamespace \

    --topic-name myTopic \

    --resource-group myRG
```

Filter messages by subject:

```
az servicebus topic subscription rule create \

    --resource-group myRG \

    --namespace-name myNamespace \

    --topic-name myTopic \

    --subscription-name mySubscription \

    --name HighPriorityOnly \

    --filter-sql-expression "priority = 'high'"
```

Comparing Event Grid and Service Bus

Feature	Event Grid	Service Bus
Latency	< 100ms	Higher (~few seconds depending on load)
Delivery	Push (HTTP/HTTPS)	Pull (AMQP, HTTP)

Ordering	No guaranteed order	FIFO with sessions
Reliability	At least once, retry on failure	At least once, dead-lettering, duplicate detection
Throughput	Very high	Moderate to high, depends on tier
Filtering	By subject, type	SQL-like rules
Use Case	Lightweight, reactive eventing	Reliable, transactional messaging

Integration Patterns

Pattern 1: Event Grid + Azure Function

A blob is uploaded → Event Grid fires → Azure Function processes and stores metadata.

Use Case: Real-time image processing.

Pattern 2: Service Bus Queue + Worker Role

A message is queued → Worker service pulls and processes the message → Acknowledges or dead-letters.

Use Case: Background order processing or billing systems.

Pattern 3: Event Grid + Service Bus

Use Event Grid to receive cloud-native events → Route to Service Bus topic for enterprise processing.

Use Case: Event fan-out with transactional requirements.

Monitoring and Diagnostics

Event Grid

- Diagnostic logs via Azure Monitor
- Dead-letter events stored in Storage Account
- Event delivery metrics (Successes, Failures, Latency)

Service Bus

- Message count, dead-letter queue size
- Throughput and latency metrics
- Activity logs and alerts for anomalies

Use Azure Monitor or Log Analytics to run queries:

```
AzureDiagnostics

| where ResourceType == "SERVICEBUSNAMESPACES"

| summarize count() by OperationName_s, StatusCode_s
```

Security and Governance

- Use **Azure RBAC** to control topic and queue access
- Enforce **network rules** with IP filtering and VNet service endpoints
- Use **Managed Identities** to authenticate apps to Service Bus
- Store secrets in **Azure Key Vault**
- Enable **Private Link** for secure, internal-only messaging

Best Practices

- Keep event payloads small and focused (Event Grid: ≤64 KB)

- Use **dead-lettering** to isolate bad messages

- Apply **retry** **policies** in subscribers

- Use **DLQ** **monitoring** to detect failures

- Batch Service Bus messages for performance

- Encrypt messages at rest and in transit (TLS 1.2+)

Conclusion

Event-driven architecture is essential for building scalable, decoupled, and reactive systems. With **Azure Event Grid** and **Azure Service Bus**, architects can implement robust communication flows that adapt to diverse operational and transactional needs.

- Use **Event Grid** for high-throughput, low-latency eventing across cloud-native components.

- Use **Service Bus** when message order, delivery guarantees, and transactional integrity are crucial.

Together, they form a powerful messaging backbone for microservices, serverless workflows, IoT, and enterprise integration in the cloud.

In the next chapter, we'll turn our focus to DevOps and Infrastructure as Code—establishing continuous integration, deployment pipelines, and automated provisioning across Azure environments.

Chapter 7: DevOps and Infrastructure as Code

CI/CD Pipelines with Azure DevOps

In the world of modern application development, agility and reliability are no longer optional—they are essential. **Continuous Integration (CI)** and **Continuous Deployment/Delivery (CD)** are foundational DevOps practices that allow teams to release features faster and more confidently. Azure DevOps provides a fully integrated suite of tools to implement CI/CD pipelines for cloud-native, hybrid, and enterprise applications hosted in Azure or elsewhere.

This section dives into building robust CI/CD pipelines using **Azure DevOps Services**, covering everything from pipeline definitions to deployment strategies, testing integrations, and best practices for automation.

Understanding CI/CD

Continuous Integration is the practice of frequently merging code changes into a shared repository and automatically validating them with tests and builds.

Continuous Deployment is the automatic release of validated builds to production. **Continuous Delivery**, on the other hand, automates everything up to production, with manual approval for the final step.

Benefits include:

- Faster time to market
- Reduced integration issues
- Increased release quality and consistency
- Automation of tedious manual tasks

Azure DevOps makes it possible to implement both CI and CD using **Pipelines**, **Repos**, **Artifacts**, **Test Plans**, and **Boards**.

Azure DevOps Overview

Azure DevOps is a set of cloud-based tools offering:

- **Azure Repos**: Git repositories with branching and pull request support

- **Azure Pipelines**: CI/CD pipelines for any platform or language

- **Azure Artifacts**: Package feeds for Maven, npm, NuGet, and more

- **Azure Boards**: Agile planning and tracking

- **Azure Test Plans**: Manual and exploratory testing

In this section, we'll focus on **Pipelines** and **Repos**.

Creating a CI Pipeline

Azure Pipelines supports both **YAML-based pipelines** (pipeline-as-code) and classic designer pipelines. YAML pipelines are preferred for versioning, portability, and automation.

Example YAML Pipeline (.azure-pipelines.yml)

```yaml
trigger:

  branches:

    include:

      - main


pool:

  vmImage: 'ubuntu-latest'


variables:

  buildConfiguration: 'Release'


steps:

- task: UseDotNet@2

  inputs:
```

```
      packageType: 'sdk'

      version: '6.0.x'

      installationPath: $(Agent.ToolsDirectory)/dotnet


- task: DotNetCoreCLI@2

  inputs:

    command: 'restore'

    projects: '**/*.csproj'


- task: DotNetCoreCLI@2

  inputs:

    command: 'build'

    arguments: '--configuration $(buildConfiguration)'

    projects: '**/*.csproj'


- task: DotNetCoreCLI@2

  inputs:

    command: 'test'

    arguments: '--configuration $(buildConfiguration)'

    projects: '**/*Tests/*.csproj'
```

This example:

1. Triggers on changes to the `main` branch.

2. Uses a Microsoft-hosted Ubuntu build agent.

3. Installs .NET 6 SDK.

4. Restores, builds, and tests the application.

Continuous Deployment with Release Pipelines

Release pipelines define **stages** such as Development, QA, Staging, and Production, allowing you to automate approval gates, environment variables, and deployment sequences.

In YAML:

```
stages:
- stage: Deploy
  jobs:
  - job: DeployApp
    pool:
      vmImage: 'ubuntu-latest'
    steps:
    - task: AzureWebApp@1
      inputs:
        azureSubscription: '<Service Connection Name>'
        appType: 'webApp'
        appName: 'myapp-dev'
        package: '$(System.DefaultWorkingDirectory)/**/*.zip'
```

In classic view:

1. Define artifact source (e.g., build output).

2. Add stages (e.g., Dev, QA, Prod).

3. Configure deployment tasks (App Service Deploy, AKS Helm Deploy, etc.).

4. Add pre-deployment approvals, triggers, and gates.

Azure Environments and Deployment Targets

Azure DevOps can deploy to:

- **Azure App Services**
- **Azure Kubernetes Service (AKS)**
- **Azure Virtual Machines**
- **Azure SQL Databases**
- **Azure Functions**
- **Non-Azure targets (via SSH, FTP, etc.)**

Azure Service Connection

To connect securely with Azure resources:

1. Go to Project Settings → Service connections.

2. Create a new connection (Azure Resource Manager).

3. Choose "Service principal (automatic)" or use a manual SPN.

Use this connection name in your pipeline YAML to authenticate and deploy.

Testing and Quality Gates

Integrate automated tests into CI pipelines to validate code and reduce regressions.

Test types:

- **Unit tests** (fast, frequent)
- **Integration tests** (dependent on services)

- **UI** **tests** (Selenium, Playwright)

Use pipeline conditions and quality gates:

```
- task: PublishTestResults@2

  inputs:

    testResultsFormat: 'JUnit'

    testResultsFiles: '**/test-results.xml'
```

Add build gates like:

- Minimum code coverage (via code coverage tools)

- Build stability history

- Manual approval steps for high-risk deployments

Secure Secrets with Azure Key Vault

Instead of storing secrets in pipeline variables, integrate Azure Key Vault:

```
- task: AzureKeyVault@2

  inputs:

    azureSubscription: '<Service Connection Name>'

    KeyVaultName: '<KeyVaultName>'

    SecretsFilter: '*'
```

Use secrets in steps via $(MySecretName).

Container-Based CI/CD

For containerized workloads:

- Use Docker or BuildKit for image builds.
- Push to Azure Container Registry (ACR) or Docker Hub.
- Deploy using Helm charts or YAML manifests.

```
- task: Docker@2
  inputs:
    command: 'buildAndPush'
    repository: 'myrepo/myapp'
    dockerfile: 'Dockerfile'
    tags: '$(Build.BuildId)'
```

Deploy to AKS using:

```
- task: Kubernetes@1
  inputs:
    connectionType: 'Azure Resource Manager'
    kubernetesServiceEndpoint: '<K8sServiceConnection>'
    namespace: 'default'
    command: 'apply'
    useConfigurationFile: true
    configuration: 'manifests/deployment.yaml'
```

Approvals and Manual Interventions

Use **approval gates** to enforce checks before moving to next stages:

- Stakeholder approval

- Security review

- Manual sign-off from QA or ops

Add via pipeline YAML or classic release editor:

```
preDeployApprovals:
  - approvers:
    - displayName: 'QA Lead'
```

Notifications and Insights

- Subscribe to build or release notifications via email or Teams.
- Use **Analytics View** for pipeline performance.
- Track failed runs, build durations, deployment frequency.

Best Practices

- Use **YAML pipelines** for versioned CI/CD definitions.
- Treat pipelines as code, stored and reviewed like application code.
- Run **linting**, **unit tests**, and **code coverage** in CI.
- Use **feature flags** to reduce release risk.
- Deploy to **sandbox environments** before production.
- Integrate with **Azure Monitor** and **App Insights** for post-deployment validation.
- Automate **rollbacks** on failure (use deployment slots or blue-green).
- Store secrets in **Key Vault**, not in pipeline variables.

Conclusion

CI/CD pipelines in Azure DevOps empower teams to release software faster, more reliably, and with fewer errors. With support for cloud-native, containerized, and hybrid deployments, Azure DevOps Pipelines can automate the entire software lifecycle—from commit to production.

By embracing a DevOps-first culture with versioned infrastructure, automated validation, secure deployments, and integrated approvals, teams not only increase agility—they reduce operational friction and improve confidence in every release.

In the next section, we'll compare ARM Templates and Bicep—Azure's native Infrastructure as Code (IaC) languages—for automating cloud infrastructure creation and management.

ARM Templates vs. Bicep

Infrastructure as Code (IaC) is a foundational DevOps practice that enables teams to automate, standardize, and version their infrastructure environments. In Azure, **Azure Resource Manager (ARM) Templates** and **Bicep** are two native IaC technologies used to define and deploy infrastructure declaratively.

This section provides a detailed comparison between ARM Templates and Bicep, explaining their syntax, structure, capabilities, use cases, and how to transition from ARM to Bicep. It includes real-world examples, best practices, and integration tips with CI/CD pipelines and policy enforcement strategies.

What Are ARM Templates?

ARM Templates are JSON-based files that define Azure resources and configurations. They are declarative, meaning you describe **what** you want, and Azure handles **how** it's provisioned.

Key Characteristics

- JSON   format

- Fully   supported   by   Azure   from   day   one

- Used   by   Microsoft   internally   for   the   Azure   Portal

- Extensive   capabilities   including   conditions,   loops,   functions

- Verbose   and   harder   to   author   without   tooling

Example ARM Template snippet:

```json
{

  "$schema":     "https://schema.management.azure.com/schemas/2019-04-01/deploymentTemplate.json#",

  "contentVersion": "1.0.0.0",

  "parameters": {

    "storageAccountName": {

      "type": "string"

    }

  },

  "resources": [

    {

      "type": "Microsoft.Storage/storageAccounts",

      "apiVersion": "2022-09-01",

      "name": "[parameters('storageAccountName')]",

      "location": "[resourceGroup().location]",

      "sku": {

        "name": "Standard_LRS"

      },

      "kind": "StorageV2",

      "properties": {}

    }

  ]

}
```

What Is Bicep?

Bicep is a domain-specific language (DSL) for ARM Template authoring. It compiles down to standard ARM JSON templates but is more concise, readable, and maintainable. It was created by Microsoft to overcome the verbosity and complexity of ARM JSON.

Key Features

- Simple, clean syntax (inspired by Terraform and HCL)

- Full parity with ARM Templates

- Modular composition via .bicep modules

- Built-in linting, IntelliSense, and tooling in VS Code

- Supports parameterization, outputs, and conditionals

- Easily converted to/from JSON ARM Templates

Example Bicep for the same storage account:

```
param storageAccountName string


resource storage 'Microsoft.Storage/storageAccounts@2022-09-01' = {

  name: storageAccountName

  location: resourceGroup().location

  sku: {

    name: 'Standard_LRS'

  }

  kind: 'StorageV2'

  properties: {}

}
```

ARM vs. Bicep: Key Comparisons

Feature	ARM Templates	Bicep
Format	JSON	Custom DSL
Readability	Verbose and complex	Clean and readable
Modularity	Via nested/deployment templates	Native module support
Tooling	Basic in VS Code	Rich IntelliSense, diagnostics
Comments	Not supported	Supported (`//`, `/* */`)
Loops and Conditions	Verbose	Clean with `for` expressions and `if`
Learning Curve	Steep for complex templates	Easier and modern syntax
Conversion Tool	Not applicable	Convert Bicep ↔ ARM via CLI
Deployment Engine	ARM (via Azure Resource Manager)	Compiles to ARM

Bicep CLI and Tooling

To install Bicep CLI:

```
az bicep install
```

Compile a Bicep file to ARM JSON:

```
az bicep build --file main.bicep
```

Decompile existing ARM to Bicep:

```
az bicep decompile --file template.json
```

Check for issues and lint:

```
az bicep build --file main.bicep --stdout
```

IntelliSense support is available in the **Bicep extension for Visual Studio Code**.

Modularization and Reusability

Bicep makes reuse simple with native support for **modules**. These are similar to Terraform modules or nested ARM templates but easier to implement.

Module Example

main.bicep

```
module storage 'modules/storage.bicep' = {

  name: 'deployStorage'

  params: {

    storageAccountName: 'mybicepstorage'

  }

}
```

modules/storage.bicep

```
param storageAccountName string
```

```
resource storage 'Microsoft.Storage/storageAccounts@2022-09-01' = {

  name: storageAccountName

  location: resourceGroup().location

  sku: {

    name: 'Standard_LRS'

  }

  kind: 'StorageV2'

  properties: {}

}
```

Modules simplify complex architectures into logical components like networks, compute, databases, and storage.

Parameters and Outputs

Bicep supports parameters with default values, allowed values, and secure strings.

```
param env string = 'dev'

param adminPassword string {

  type: 'securestring'

}


output location string = resourceGroup().location
```

You can pass parameters via:

- Parameter   files   (parameters.dev.json)

- Inline   CLI   values

- Azure Pipelines or GitHub Actions secrets

Deployment Options

Use the Azure CLI or PowerShell for deployments:

```
az deployment group create \

  --resource-group myRG \

  --template-file main.bicep \

  --parameters storageAccountName=mybicepstore
```

For subscriptions, management groups, and tenants:

```
az deployment sub create \

  --location eastus \

  --template-file main.bicep
```

These deployments are idempotent: repeated executions only apply changes.

CI/CD Integration

Bicep files can be integrated into CI/CD pipelines using Azure DevOps or GitHub Actions.

Azure DevOps Example

```
trigger:

- main


pool:

  vmImage: 'ubuntu-latest'
```

```
steps:

- task: AzureCLI@2

  inputs:

    azureSubscription: 'my-service-connection'

    scriptType: bash

    scriptLocation: inlineScript

    inlineScript: |

      az bicep install

      az deployment group create \

        --resource-group myRG \

        --template-file main.bicep \

        --parameters storageAccountName=mybicepstore
```

Security and Governance

- Store secrets (e.g., admin passwords, keys) in Azure Key Vault.
- Use **Azure Policy** to enforce standards (e.g., allowed regions).
- Apply **resource locks** to prevent accidental deletion.
- Use **role-based access control (RBAC)** for deployment permissions.
- Scan templates with **Bicep Linter** and **PSRule for Azure**.

Transitioning from ARM to Bicep

For existing ARM users, transitioning to Bicep is straightforward.

1. **Decompile** existing JSON templates to Bicep.

2. **Refactor** into reusable modules.

3. **Integrate** into version control and CI/CD.

4. **Train** teams on Bicep syntax and tooling.

```
az bicep decompile --file old-template.json --out new-template.bicep
```

The Bicep learning curve is gentle, making it an ideal candidate for long-term infrastructure automation.

Best Practices

- Use **modules** for repeated patterns.

- Keep **main.bicep** files focused—delegate details to modules.

- Use **parameter files** to manage environment-specific values.

- Secure all secrets using **Key Vault references**.

- Validate templates with `az deployment what-if` before applying.

- Enable **linting and diagnostics** in your CI/CD workflows.

- Store all templates and modules in **version control**.

- Adopt **GitOps** and **Infrastructure Drift Detection** strategies.

Conclusion

Both ARM Templates and Bicep offer robust ways to define infrastructure declaratively, but Bicep's modern, readable syntax and native tooling make it the recommended approach for most scenarios today. Bicep provides full ARM Template parity with better modularization, developer experience, and maintainability.

As Azure evolves, Bicep continues to gain features and community support, making it the default choice for automating Azure infrastructure deployments at scale. In the next section, we'll explore using **Terraform**, a popular multi-cloud Infrastructure as Code tool, in Azure environments for even greater flexibility and open-source integration.

Terraform on Azure

As organizations scale their infrastructure and adopt hybrid or multi-cloud strategies, many turn to **Terraform**, an open-source Infrastructure as Code (IaC) tool developed by HashiCorp. Terraform allows you to define, provision, and manage infrastructure using a consistent CLI workflow and a declarative language known as **HashiCorp Configuration Language (HCL)**.

Terraform works across cloud providers—including Azure, AWS, Google Cloud, and many more—making it ideal for teams seeking platform-agnostic tooling. Azure supports Terraform natively, and Microsoft maintains the official **Azure Provider**, ensuring tight integration with ARM and Azure services.

This section explores how to use Terraform with Azure, including provider configuration, state management, common patterns, security considerations, and how to integrate Terraform into your CI/CD workflows for complete infrastructure automation.

Why Terraform?

Terraform provides benefits such as:

- **Cloud-agnostic**: Manage Azure and other cloud environments using the same tool and language.

- **Modular and reusable**: Organize infrastructure into reusable modules.

- **Declarative syntax**: Define what infrastructure should exist.

- **Plan and apply**: Preview changes before applying them.

- **State management**: Track the current state of infrastructure.

- **Open ecosystem**: Use community and verified modules.

Terraform is especially valuable when managing complex environments or integrating multiple services and systems across different providers.

Terraform Basics

Terraform code is written in **.tf** files using HCL. A basic structure includes:

- **Providers**: Plugins that enable interaction with APIs.
- **Resources**: Declarative definitions of infrastructure (VMs, networks, etc.).
- **Variables**: Parameterize and customize your code.
- **Outputs**: Share values from one module/environment to another.
- **Modules**: Packages of Terraform configurations.

Example:

```
provider "azurerm" {

  features {}

}


resource "azurerm_resource_group" "example" {

  name     = "myResourceGroup"

  location = "eastus"

}
```

Setting Up Terraform with Azure

Step 1: Install Terraform

Terraform CLI can be downloaded from the official website. Once installed, verify with:

```
terraform version
```

Step 2: Authenticate with Azure

Terraform supports several authentication methods:

- Azure CLI authentication (recommended for local dev):

```
az login
```

- Service principal (for automation):

```
az ad sp create-for-rbac --role="Contributor" --
scopes="/subscriptions/<subscription_id>"
```

Use environment variables or `provider` block configuration for automation.

Basic Terraform Workflow

Terraform follows a three-step cycle:

1. **terraform init** – Initializes the working directory and downloads provider plugins.

2. **terraform plan** – Shows what actions Terraform will perform.

3. **terraform apply** – Applies the planned changes to real infrastructure.

```
terraform init

terraform plan

terraform apply
```

To destroy resources:

```
terraform destroy
```

Azure Resource Example

```
provider "azurerm" {

  features {}
```

```
}


resource "azurerm_storage_account" "example" {

  name                      = "mytfstorageacct"

  resource_group_name       = "myResourceGroup"

  location                  = "eastus"

  account_tier              = "Standard"

  account_replication_type  = "LRS"

}
```

To parameterize, use variables:

```
variable "location" {

  default = "eastus"

}


resource "azurerm_resource_group" "main" {

  name     = "demo-rg"

  location = var.location

}
```

Managing State in Azure

Terraform uses a **state file** to track your deployed resources. You can store this state remotely using **Azure Storage** for collaboration and security.

Create storage account and container:

```
az storage account create --name tfstateaccount --resource-group myRG
--location eastus --sku Standard_LRS

az   storage   container   create   --name   tfstate   --account-name
tfstateaccount
```

Configure backend in Terraform:

```
terraform {

  backend "azurerm" {

    resource_group_name   = "myRG"

    storage_account_name = "tfstateaccount"

    container_name        = "tfstate"

    key                   = "terraform.tfstate"

  }

}
```

Then run:

```
terraform init
```

This securely stores and locks state to avoid race conditions.

Terraform Modules

Modules allow you to encapsulate and reuse infrastructure code.

Create a Module

modules/network/main.tf:

```
resource "azurerm_virtual_network" "vnet" {

  name                = var.vnet_name
```

```
  address_space       = var.address_space

  location            = var.location

  resource_group_name = var.resource_group_name

}
```

Use it in your main configuration:

```
module "vnet" {

  source              = "./modules/network"

  vnet_name           = "myVNet"

  address_space       = ["10.0.0.0/16"]

  location            = "eastus"

  resource_group_name = "myRG"

}
```

Modules promote consistency and best practices across teams and projects.

Integration with CI/CD

Terraform fits well into DevOps pipelines, such as Azure DevOps and GitHub Actions.

GitHub Actions Example

```
name: Terraform


on:

  push:

    branches:

      - main
```

```yaml
jobs:
  terraform:
    runs-on: ubuntu-latest

    steps:
    - uses: actions/checkout@v3
    - name: Set up Terraform
      uses: hashicorp/setup-terraform@v3

    - name: Terraform Init
      run: terraform init

    - name: Terraform Plan
      run: terraform plan

    - name: Terraform Apply
      run: terraform apply -auto-approve
      env:
        ARM_CLIENT_ID: ${{ secrets.ARM_CLIENT_ID }}
        ARM_CLIENT_SECRET: ${{ secrets.ARM_CLIENT_SECRET }}
        ARM_SUBSCRIPTION_ID: ${{ secrets.ARM_SUBSCRIPTION_ID }}
        ARM_TENANT_ID: ${{ secrets.ARM_TENANT_ID }}
```

Secrets can be configured in GitHub for secure authentication.

Security and Policy Integration

- Use **environment variables** or secure vaults to manage credentials.

- Use **Terraform Cloud/Enterprise** for policy enforcement and team management.

- Integrate **Azure Policy** and **Sentinel (in Terraform Cloud)** for compliance.

- Enable **lock files** (`.terraform.lock.hcl`) for deterministic builds.

- Scan code with tools like **tflint**, **tfsec**, or **Checkov** for static analysis.

Common Patterns

- **Environment Separation**: Use workspaces or separate state files per environment.

- **State Locking**: Always use remote state with locking for teams.

- **Immutable Infrastructure**: Avoid in-place changes—replace resources when needed.

- **Secrets Management**: Use Azure Key Vault with data sources:

```
data "azurerm_key_vault_secret" "adminpassword" {
  name         = "adminPassword"
  key_vault_id = azurerm_key_vault.main.id
}
```

- **Variable Files**: Use `.tfvars` files per environment for customization.

Best Practices

- Structure code using folders for `modules`, `envs`, and `main`.

- Use **locals** to reduce repetition.

- Version control everything, including state backends and modules.

- Document each module's purpose and inputs/outputs.

- Validate (`terraform validate`) and format (`terraform fmt`) before committing.

- Use `terraform plan -out plan.tfplan` for approval gates.

- Tag all resources with metadata (owner, purpose, environment).

- Automate drift detection and reconciliation.

- Rotate credentials and restrict permissions via RBAC and least privilege.

Conclusion

Terraform is a powerful and flexible Infrastructure as Code tool that allows teams to manage Azure infrastructure with consistency, version control, and automation. Its declarative syntax, modular structure, and broad ecosystem make it a top choice for enterprise-scale and multi-cloud environments.

Whether used independently or alongside Azure-native tooling like Bicep, Terraform offers the capabilities required for modern cloud operations. In the next section, we'll dive into deployment observability, focusing on how to monitor deployments and roll back changes using tools like Azure Monitor, Application Insights, and deployment history tracking.

Monitoring Deployments and Rollbacks

A mature DevOps practice is not complete without robust monitoring and rollback strategies. While CI/CD pipelines help you deploy quickly, observability ensures that deployments are healthy, performant, and traceable. Equally important is the ability to **rollback** when failures occur, either automatically or with minimal intervention.

In this section, we explore how to monitor deployments and implement rollbacks in Azure environments using native services like **Azure Monitor**, **Application Insights**, **Deployment Center**, **Release Pipelines**, **Container Insights**, and **deployment slots**. We'll also examine how logging, metrics, alerts, and integration with incident management tools can help you build resilient and observable systems.

Deployment Observability: The What and Why

Observability is the practice of instrumenting infrastructure and applications so that teams can understand and debug their behavior in real time.

Key observability goals in deployment:

- Confirm the deployment occurred as expected
- Monitor application health and performance
- Detect regressions, errors, and performance degradation
- Track deployment history and changes
- Roll back fast when something breaks

In Azure, observability spans **infrastructure-level telemetry**, **application-level insights**, and **pipeline-level tracking**.

Azure Monitor

Azure Monitor is the unified platform for collecting and analyzing operational telemetry in Azure. It includes:

- **Metrics**: Quantitative data such as CPU usage, latency, memory
- **Logs**: Event and trace data from services and applications
- **Alerts**: Real-time notification and action triggers
- **Workbooks**: Dashboards and data visualizations

Use it to monitor:

- Resource health and uptime
- Deployment frequency and duration
- Error spikes after a deployment
- Changes to infrastructure state

Example: Create an alert for deployment failure

```
az monitor metrics alert create \

  --name "DeploymentFailureAlert" \

  --resource-group "myRG" \

  --scopes                              "/subscriptions/<sub-
id>/resourceGroups/myRG/providers/Microsoft.Web/sites/myApp" \

  --condition "total Requests > 100 where ResponseCode == 500" \

  --description "Trigger on surge of 500 errors post deployment"
```

Application Insights

Application Insights is part of Azure Monitor and provides deep insight into application-level performance and user behavior.

It supports:

- Request   traces
- Exception   tracking
- Dependency   maps
- Custom   events   and   metrics
- Live   metrics   stream

To correlate deployments with performance, use **custom telemetry** or **deployment annotations**.

Example: Annotate deployment in Application Insights

```
$aiAppId = "<app-insights-app-id>"

$aiKey = "<instrumentation-key>"

Invoke-RestMethod -Method POST `

  -Uri  "https://api.applicationinsights.io/v1/apps/$aiAppId/events"
```

```
-Headers @{ "x-api-key" = $aiKey } `

-Body (@{

  name = "Deployment"

  time = (Get-Date).ToString("o")

  iKey = $aiKey

  data = @{

    baseType = "EventData"

    baseData = @{

      name = "ReleaseDeployed"

      properties = @{

        version = "1.0.2"

        environment = "Production"

      }

    }

  }

} | ConvertTo-Json -Depth 10)
```

This allows you to overlay deployment events on application performance charts.

Deployment History and Audit Logs

Azure resources include **deployment history** under Resource Group settings. Each ARM or Bicep deployment logs:

• What	template	was	used
• When	the	deployment	occurred
• Which	resources	were	affected

- Who initiated it
- Status (Succeeded, Failed, Canceled)

Access via Portal, CLI, or REST:

```
az deployment group show \
  --name myDeployment \
  --resource-group myRG
```

Use **Azure Activity Log** and **Audit Logs** for compliance and traceability.

Deployment Slots and Blue-Green Deployments

For **zero-downtime deployments**, use **deployment slots** (especially with Azure App Service):

- Deploy to staging slot
- Validate deployment (manual or scripted checks)
- Swap with production slot

This provides a quick rollback path:

```
az webapp deployment slot swap \
  --name myApp \
  --resource-group myRG \
  --slot staging \
  --target-slot production
```

For **blue-green deployments**:

- Blue is the current version

- Green is the new version
- Traffic is switched over after testing green
- Revert to blue in case of issues

Canary Deployments

In **canary deployments**, a small portion of users receive the new version first. Monitor their behavior before full rollout.

Azure Front Door and **Azure Traffic Manager** can split traffic by weight or rules:

```
az network traffic-manager endpoint update \

  --resource-group myRG \

  --profile-name myTrafficProfile \

  --name canaryEndpoint \

  --type externalEndpoints \

  --weight 10
```

Adjust weight dynamically to increase exposure gradually.

Rollback Strategies

Rolling back can be:

- **Manual** (use previous pipeline artifact)
- **Automated** (triggered by health checks or alerts)
- **Slot-based** (swap to staging slot)
- **Version-controlled** (redeploy known-good release)

In Azure Pipelines:

```
- task: AzureCLI@2

  inputs:

    scriptType: bash

    scriptLocation: inlineScript

    inlineScript: |

      if [ "$DEPLOYMENT_STATUS" != "Succeeded" ]; then

        echo "Rolling back..."

        az webapp deployment slot swap \

          --name myApp \

          --resource-group myRG \

          --slot staging \

          --target-slot production

      fi
```

Always ensure rollback artifacts (e.g., container image versions, previous ARM templates) are retained.

Real-Time Monitoring and Alerting

Set up **custom alerts** based on post-deployment indicators:

- Request/response   time   spikes

- Error   rates   above   threshold

- CPU/memory   anomalies

- Application   crashes

Alerts can notify via:

- Email

- SMS

- Microsoft   Teams   or   Slack

- Azure   Logic   Apps   or   Functions

Example alert with Action Group:

```
az monitor action-group create \

  --resource-group myRG \

  --name DevOpsAlerts \

  --action email admin admin@company.com
```

Logging and Telemetry

Use **Log Analytics** to query and analyze deployment data across environments:

```
AppTraces

| where TimeGenerated > ago(1h)

| where Message contains "deployment"

| summarize count() by Message, Level
```

Instrument your pipelines to send **custom logs** or **structured events** for each stage.

GitOps and Deployment Drift

With GitOps, desired state is defined in Git, and agents (e.g., Flux, ArgoCD) reconcile live state.

Benefits:

- Audit trail of changes
- Easy rollback via Git reversion
- Drift detection and correction

Monitor drift with tools like:

- **Terraform Plan in CI**
- **ARM/Bicep what-if deployment**
- **Azure Resource Graph** queries for configuration state

Integrating with Incident Management

Use services like:

- **Azure Sentinel**: For security incidents
- **ServiceNow**, **PagerDuty**, **Opsgenie**: For automated alert escalation
- **Microsoft Teams bots**: To approve or reject deployment rollbacks

Example: Logic App triggered on critical alert → notify on Teams → trigger rollback pipeline if approved.

Best Practices

- Use **annotated deployments** for better correlation.
- Monitor **key performance indicators (KPIs)** before and after deployments.
- Use **deployment gates** (health probes, alerts, tests) before completing rollout.
- Always test rollback paths during staging.
- Automate **chaos testing** and failure injection to validate recovery.
- Retain **deployment artifacts** and templates for previous versions.

- Visualize deployments using **workbooks** and **Grafana dashboards**.

- Use **feature flags** to reduce deployment risk without rollback.

Conclusion

Deployment observability and rollback readiness are non-negotiable in modern DevOps. Azure provides a rich ecosystem—from deployment slots and canary rollouts to full-stack monitoring and alerting—allowing teams to deploy with confidence.

By proactively measuring health, automating rollbacks, and integrating alerts into operations workflows, you build not only a fast pipeline but a safe one. The result is higher release velocity, reduced downtime, and more resilient applications.

In the next chapter, we'll turn to cost management—understanding Azure's pricing models, cost forecasting, resource optimization, and budgeting techniques to ensure your infrastructure is not only scalable but also financially sustainable.

Chapter 8: Cost Management and Optimization

Understanding Azure Pricing Models

Cost is a central consideration in any cloud architecture. As cloud adoption grows, organizations must move beyond simply provisioning resources—they must ensure that every dollar spent is delivering measurable value. Microsoft Azure provides flexible pricing models tailored for diverse workloads, but understanding them requires attention to detail.

This section delves into the different pricing models Azure offers, how billing is calculated, resource-specific cost structures, common cost drivers, and strategies for choosing the right pricing options based on business needs. By mastering these fundamentals, you can design architectures that are not only performant and secure—but also cost-efficient and scalable over time.

Core Azure Pricing Principles

At a foundational level, Azure pricing is based on a **pay-as-you-go** model with additional options for **reserved instances**, **spot pricing**, and **commitment plans**. Charges are based on **resource consumption**, such as:

- Compute   hours

- Storage   volume

- Network   traffic

- API   calls

- Reserved   capacity

Azure also charges **per second**, **per minute**, or **per transaction**, depending on the service.

Key Factors Influencing Cost:

- Region: Pricing varies by region due to data center costs.

- Service Tier: Higher tiers (e.g., Premium, P3v3) cost more but offer better performance.

- Provisioning Model: Always-on vs. auto-scaled services.

- Licensing: Licensing-included or BYOL (Bring Your Own License) for SQL Server, Windows, etc.

- Availability: HA features like Availability Zones or GRS for storage increase cost.

Compute Pricing Models

Virtual Machines (VMs)

Pricing for VMs depends on:

- Size (CPU, RAM, disk)

- Operating system (Linux is cheaper than Windows)

- Region

- Disk type (Standard HDD, Standard SSD, Premium SSD)

- Usage duration

Pricing model options:

1. **Pay-As-You-Go**: Billed per second, no commitment.

2. **Reserved Instances (RI)**: 1- or 3-year commitments with up to 72% savings.

3. **Spot Instances**: Deeply discounted unused capacity, but with eviction risk.

```
az vm list-skus --location eastus --output table
```

Use Spot VMs for stateless batch processing and development/test environments.

App Service Pricing

App Services are priced based on the selected **App Service Plan** tier:

- Free/Shared: Limited features, shared compute.

- Basic: Dedicated compute, manual scaling.

- Standard: Auto-scaling, staging slots, daily backups.

- PremiumV3: High performance, scale-out, VNet integration.

Pricing is calculated per instance/hour.

Containers and Serverless

Azure Kubernetes Service (AKS)

You only pay for the **worker nodes** (VMs), not the control plane.

- Cost depends on node size, OS, and disk type.
- Use node auto-scaling to optimize consumption.

Azure Container Apps

Charged based on:

- Number of requests
- vCPU and memory allocated per second
- Concurrent execution time

Azure Functions

Azure Functions uses a **consumption-based** pricing model:

- First 1 million executions/month free.
- Billed per execution + resource consumption (GB-s, vCPU-s).

Premium and Dedicated plans are available for always-on or higher performance needs.

Example monthly cost formula:

```
Total cost = Executions * Price per execution + GB-s used * Rate +
vCPU-s * Rate
```

Storage Pricing Models

Azure storage offers several redundancy and performance tiers:

Tier	Redundancy Options	Use Case
Hot	LRS, ZRS, GRS	Frequently accessed data
Cool	LRS, ZRS, GRS	Infrequently accessed, ≥30-day retention
Archive	LRS, GRS	Rare access, ≥180-day retention

Pricing includes:

- Storage capacity (per GB/month)
- Operations (PUT, GET, LIST)
- Data retrieval (Archive/Cool)
- Data egress (internet)

Archive retrieval incurs delayed access and higher costs.

Database Pricing

Azure SQL Database

Options include:

- **DTU-based**: Bundled compute/storage (older model).
- **vCore-based**: Separates compute and storage, supports reserved pricing and HA.

vCore tiers:

- General Purpose

- Business Critical

- Hyperscale

Serverless is available in the vCore model, where billing is paused during inactivity.

Cosmos DB

Pricing depends on:

- Provisioned throughput (RU/s)

- Storage used

- Request units per operation

- Consistency level

- Multi-region replication

Serverless and Autoscale options allow for flexibility in unpredictable workloads.

Networking Costs

Not all network traffic is free. You are charged for:

- **Egress**: Data leaving Azure (e.g., to the internet, other regions)

- **VPN Gateway**: Hourly rate + data transfer

- **ExpressRoute**: Monthly fee + data transfer

- **Load Balancer**: Standard tier has per-rule and data processed charges

- **Azure Front Door / CDN**: Per GB data served + request count

Azure VNet peering is typically free for inbound, but outbound cross-region incurs a charge.

Example:

```
Outbound to Internet: $0.087 per GB (first 5 GB free)
```

```
VNet Peering (intra-region): Free

VNet Peering (inter-region): $0.01-$0.035 per GB
```

Licensing and Hybrid Benefits

Azure offers cost savings via **Azure Hybrid Benefit**:

- Bring your own licenses for Windows Server or SQL Server.
- Applies to VMs, SQL Database, Synapse, and more.
- Combine with Reserved Instances for compounded savings.

Enable Hybrid Benefit when creating a VM:

```
az vm create \

  --name myVM \

  --resource-group myRG \

  --image win2022datacenter \

  --license-type Windows_Server
```

Use **Cost Calculator** and **Pricing Calculator** to estimate savings.

Cost Optimization Features in Azure

Azure provides several tools to help you understand and manage cost:

- **Azure Pricing Calculator**: Interactive tool for estimating monthly costs.
- **Azure TCO Calculator**: Compare on-premises vs. Azure-based TCO.
- **Azure Cost Management + Billing**:
  - View usage and cost trends.

- ○ Analyze per-resource, per-subscription, or per-tag cost.

- ○ Export usage data to CSV or Power BI.

Billing Structures and Subscriptions

Azure bills at the **subscription level**, broken down into:

- Resource groups

- Tags

- Management groups (for enterprise accounts)

You can:

- Apply **tags** for cost attribution (e.g., `costcenter:marketing`)

- Group resources under **management groups**

- Use **Enterprise Agreements (EA)** for large-scale, unified billing

---

Example Scenario: Web App Cost Breakdown

Assume a medium-tier architecture:

- App Service Plan: Standard S1 (1 instance)

- Azure SQL Database: General Purpose (2 vCores)

- Storage Account: 100 GB hot tier

- Application Insights: 2 GB logs/month

- Azure CDN: 100 GB egress/month

Approximate monthly cost:

- App Service: $74.40

- SQL DB: $186

- Storage: $2.00

- App Insights: $4.20

- CDN: $8.70

Total: ~$275/month

By moving to Reserved SQL, you could save ~$70/month.

Best Practices for Pricing Management

- Always **estimate cost** before provisioning.

- Choose the **right region** based on pricing and compliance.

- Use **reserved capacity** where workloads are predictable.

- Enable **Auto-shutdown** for non-production VMs.

- Use **serverless** and **consumption** models for bursty workloads.

- Monitor with **Azure Cost Management**.

- Apply **tags** consistently to track spend.

- Conduct **cost reviews** monthly with finance/stakeholders.

- Set **budgets and alerts** to prevent overspend.

Conclusion

Understanding Azure pricing models is foundational to designing financially responsible cloud solutions. From virtual machines and databases to serverless functions and CDN traffic, every resource type has unique cost considerations. By taking advantage of Azure's pricing calculators, hybrid benefits, and reserved capacity options, you can significantly reduce expenses without compromising performance or scalability.

In the next section, we'll explore tools and techniques for estimating costs and implementing cost-efficient architectural practices—from early-stage planning through production-scale operations.

Cost Estimation Tools and Best Practices

Estimating costs before deploying Azure resources is a critical part of effective architecture planning. It ensures alignment with business budgets, prevents unexpected billing surprises, and provides clarity for stakeholders evaluating the financial impact of proposed solutions. Azure offers a comprehensive suite of cost estimation tools, including the **Azure Pricing Calculator**, **TCO Calculator**, and **Cost Management**. Used together with proper architectural foresight and tagging practices, these tools allow organizations to forecast, allocate, and optimize cloud spending.

This section provides a deep dive into these cost estimation tools, how to use them efficiently, and a framework of best practices to integrate cost-awareness into every phase of cloud architecture design and operation.

The Importance of Cost Estimation in Cloud Architecture

Unlike traditional data centers with fixed upfront capital expenses, Azure and other cloud platforms use **operational expenditure (OpEx)** models. While OpEx enables flexibility and scale, it also demands **proactive estimation** and **budget control**.

Reasons cost estimation is essential:

- **Business Justification**: Stakeholders require cost projections for approvals.

- **Compliance and Audit**: Budget forecasting is part of governance and financial planning.

- **Project Planning**: Accurate estimates inform resource allocation and delivery timelines.

- **TCO Comparison**: Comparing Azure to on-premises or other clouds for cost justification.

- **Optimization**: Enables identification of cost drivers early in the design process.

Azure Pricing Calculator

The **Azure Pricing Calculator** (https://azure.com/pricing/calculator) is the primary tool for estimating costs of Azure services before deployment.

Key Features

- Add   multiple   services   to   the   same   estimate

- Customize resource specifications (e.g., VM size, disk type, location)
- Choose billing options (e.g., pay-as-you-go, reserved instances)
- Estimate monthly costs with itemized breakdown
- Save, share, or export estimates for review

Example: Estimating a Web Application Stack

1. Select "App Service" from the calculator.
2. Choose "Standard S1" plan, set to 1 instance, East US.
3. Add "Azure SQL Database," select "General Purpose," 2 vCores, 32 GB storage.
4. Add "Storage Account," with 100 GB in Hot tier.
5. Choose "Application Insights," 2 GB ingestion/month.

Result: An estimate of ~$275/month with flexibility to adjust per region, tier, or quantity.

This transparency helps teams align on architecture cost trade-offs.

Azure TCO Calculator

The **Total Cost of Ownership (TCO) Calculator** (https://azure.com/tco) compares the cost of running workloads on-premises versus in Azure.

Steps to Use:

1. Enter current infrastructure details:
   - Number of servers
   - Storage requirements
   - Licensing (Windows, SQL)
   - Power/cooling costs
2. Customize assumptions:
   - Maintenance cost %

- ○ VM density
- ○ Support staff

3. View comparison report:

- ○ 3-year total cost breakdown
- ○ Savings percentage
- ○ Payback period

This is particularly useful during migration discussions to justify cloud investments.

Azure Cost Management + Billing

Once services are deployed, **Cost Management + Billing** provides:

- **Historical usage** data (daily granularity)
- **Forecasted costs** based on trends
- **Resource-level** spend analysis
- **Tag-based** cost allocation
- **Export** to CSV or Power BI
- **Budgets** and alerts

Use it alongside estimates to validate actual usage against forecasts and refine future planning.

Power BI for Cost Visualization

Export cost data to Power BI for customized dashboards:

1. In Cost Management, go to "Exports" → Schedule a daily export.

2. Configure Power BI to import the CSV file.

3. Create visuals for:

- Cost by service
- Cost by resource group
- Cost trend over time
- Forecast vs. actual variance

Power BI empowers financial teams to track and report on cloud spend with precision.

Best Practices for Cost Estimation

1. Always Estimate Before Deployment

Make cost estimation a **precondition** for any new workload. Include it in architecture review checklists and DevOps workflows.

2. Use Tags in Estimates and Deployments

Define tags like:

- `environment:` `production`
- `costcenter:` `marketing`
- `project:` `website-redesign`

Estimate based on these dimensions and ensure the same tags are applied to actual resources.

3. Align with Resource Lifecycle Plans

When estimating cost, factor in:

- **Provisioning timelines**: Pre-prod vs. production phases
- **Usage intensity**: 24/7 vs. 9-to-5 workloads
- **Expected growth**: Scale projections over 6–12 months
- **Auto-scaling policies**: Minimum/maximum instance counts

Don't estimate only the day-one cost—plan for full lifecycle TCO.

4. Evaluate Cost Options Per Service

Each Azure service has pricing variations. Consider:

- VM: Pay-as-you-go vs. Reserved vs. Spot
- SQL DB: vCore vs. DTU, Single vs. Elastic Pool
- Storage: Hot vs. Cool vs. Archive
- Functions: Consumption vs. Premium Plan
- App Service: Basic vs. PremiumV3

Compare each using the calculator's side-by-side price matrix.

5. Maintain Versioned Estimates

Treat cost estimates like code:

- Save them in a central repository (e.g., Git)
- Version them alongside infrastructure code
- Tag versions based on environment or approval cycle

This provides traceability and supports governance audits.

6. Include Networking and Egress

A common mistake is ignoring **egress traffic**, especially in:

- CDN and Azure Front Door usage
- Cross-region replication (e.g., GRS Storage)
- VNet-to-VNet peering
- Internet-bound data

Estimate outbound data in GB and include it in pricing scenarios.

7. Factor in Operational Costs

Many tools/services incur **usage-based** operational charges:

- Azure Monitor: Data ingestion and retention
- Defender for Cloud: Per-node protection charges
- Azure Automation: Per job run/minute of usage
- API Management: Request count and throughput tiers

Make sure these are included in service layer estimations.

8. Use Conditional Scenarios for Options

Model different scenarios for stakeholders:

- Best case vs. average vs. peak usage
- Regional pricing differences (East US vs. UK South)
- High availability vs. standard deployment
- Multicloud comparison (Azure vs. AWS vs. GCP)

Automating Cost Estimation

For large-scale or repeatable scenarios, consider programmatic estimation:

- **Pricing API**: Retrieve real-time service rates
- **Terraform/Bicep output estimators**: Export resource lists for pricing import
- **Azure Cost CLI**: Use `az consumption` commands for usage data

Example:

```
az consumption usage list --start-date 2025-04-01 --end-date 2025-04-
21 --output table
```

Automate comparison against budget thresholds with scripts or alerts.

Educating Stakeholders

Include cost estimation in:

- **Sprint planning**: For each new feature or service

- **Architecture** **design** **documents**

- **Review meetings**: Share visuals from Pricing Calculator or Cost Management

- **Documentation**: Maintain cost model diagrams

This fosters a **cost-aware culture**, crucial in agile and DevOps environments.

Conclusion

Cost estimation is not a one-time task—it's a continuous practice that starts in the planning phase and continues throughout the deployment lifecycle. Azure provides powerful tools like the Pricing Calculator, TCO Calculator, and Cost Management to help teams stay ahead of their cloud budgets.

When used with proper tagging, forecasting, and collaboration, these tools enable a culture of transparency and financial accountability. Accurate and proactive cost estimation ensures that cloud solutions remain aligned with business goals, avoid financial risk, and scale sustainably over time.

In the next section, we'll focus on resource-level optimization techniques—right-sizing, scheduling, auto-scaling, and intelligent service selection—to minimize waste and maximize the return on your Azure investment.

Optimizing Resource Utilization

Effective cost management in Azure goes beyond accurate estimation—it requires **active optimization** of deployed resources. As applications evolve and workloads shift, Azure environments often accumulate **inefficiencies**, such as overprovisioned virtual machines, idle services, underutilized storage, or unnecessarily high availability configurations.

This section provides a deep dive into the strategies, tools, and architectural techniques for optimizing resource utilization in Azure. We will explore automation, rightsizing, scheduling, scaling, and monitoring approaches that reduce unnecessary spend without compromising performance, availability, or security.

Why Resource Optimization Matters

Cloud architecture allows for rapid provisioning and scalability—but without governance, costs can spiral out of control. Optimization is essential to:

- Eliminate wasted resources
- Align performance with real usage
- Ensure cost-efficient scaling
- Improve environmental sustainability (green computing)
- Create predictable financial operations

Resource optimization is both a technical and financial practice that must be **continuous**—not a one-time review.

Common Areas of Overprovisioning

1. **Virtual Machines (VMs)**
   - Oversized VMs (CPU, RAM)
   - Running non-production VMs 24/7
   - Low utilization or idling VMs
   - Inefficient disk types (Premium when Standard is sufficient)

2. **App Services and Functions**
   - Premium or isolated tiers for small apps
   - Always-on settings in test environments
   - Unused deployment slots

3. **Databases**
   - Over-provisioned vCores or DTUs
   - Long-running databases with minimal queries
   - High redundancy for non-critical apps

4. **Storage**

   - Premium SSDs on infrequent access workloads
   - Old blobs or unmanaged snapshots
   - Over-retained logs and backups

5. **Networking**

   - Idle public IPs
   - ExpressRoute circuits with low throughput
   - Over-provisioned Application Gateways

Optimization Strategy Framework

To optimize resource utilization systematically, apply the following framework:

1. **Monitor and Analyze**

   - Identify idle or underutilized resources
   - Use tools like Azure Advisor, Monitor, and Cost Management

2. **Right-size**

   - Adjust sizes based on actual usage patterns

3. **Automate**

   - Schedule shutdowns and autoscaling
   - Use serverless where feasible

4. **Decommission**

   - Remove unused resources and stale deployments

5. **Re-evaluate SKUs**

   - Reconsider pricing tiers and storage types

6. **Re-architect**

   ○ Migrate   to   managed   or   serverless   services

Using Azure Advisor

Azure Advisor provides actionable recommendations for optimization across:

- Cost

- Performance

- Security

- Reliability

- Operational   Excellence

To access:

```
az advisor recommendation list --output table
```

Key cost-saving recommendations include:

- Downsize   underutilized   VMs

- Delete   idle   public   IPs

- Consolidate   unused   SQL   DBs

- Remove   unattached   disks

Each recommendation includes **estimated monthly savings** and links to automate remediation.

Rightsizing Virtual Machines

Rightsizing is the practice of matching VM resources (CPU, RAM, disk) to actual workload demand.

Steps to Rightsize:

1. Enable **Azure Monitor** and **Log Analytics** to collect metrics.

2. Review CPU and memory utilization over 14–30 days.

3. Identify VMs with consistent usage below 20–30%.

4. Switch to a smaller size in the same VM family.

5. Redeploy or resize using CLI or portal.

Example:

```
az vm resize \

  --resource-group myRG \

  --name myVM \

  --size Standard_B2s
```

For production, use **Availability Zones** or VM Scale Sets for flexibility in scaling without overprovisioning.

Scheduling and Automation

Non-production environments often run continuously when they don't need to.

Use **Azure Automation**, **Logic Apps**, or **Azure DevTest Labs** to **schedule shutdown/startup** of resources.

Example Automation Account schedule:

```
Start-AzVM -ResourceGroupName "myRG" -Name "devVM"

Stop-AzVM -ResourceGroupName "myRG" -Name "devVM" -Force
```

Create schedules for:

- Dev/test   VMs

- QA and staging environments
- Auto-stop idle App Services

Combine with **Runbooks** for full environment lifecycle control.

Leveraging Auto-Scaling

App Services

Enable built-in **auto-scale rules**:

```
az monitor autoscale create \

  --resource-group myRG \

  --resource myAppServicePlan \

  --resource-type "Microsoft.Web/serverfarms" \

  --name autoscaleWebApp \

  --min-count 1 --max-count 5 --count 2
```

Add scale-out rules based on:

- CPU > 70%
- HTTP request count > 500
- Custom metrics (queue length, memory)

Virtual Machine Scale Sets (VMSS)

Scale VMs in and out based on usage patterns:

```
az vmss create \

  --resource-group myRG \

  --name myScaleSet \

  --image UbuntuLTS \
```

```
--admin-username azureuser \

--generate-ssh-keys
```

Use built-in autoscale profiles or integrate with Azure Monitor metrics.

Azure Functions and Container Apps

These **scale automatically** by default. Use them wherever workloads are bursty or event-driven to reduce idle costs.

Optimizing Databases

Azure SQL Database

- Switch from provisioned to **serverless** for intermittent workloads.

- Scale down vCores in off-peak hours using **Elastic Jobs** or **PowerShell**.

- Use **Elastic Pools** for shared resources across small databases.

```
az sql db update \

  --name mydb \

  --resource-group myRG \

  --server myserver \

  --compute-model Serverless
```

Cosmos DB

- Enable **Autoscale** to adjust RU/s based on demand.

- Review **partitioning** **strategy** to avoid hotspots.

- Use **analytical** **storage** for cost-efficient analytics.

Intelligent Storage Optimization

1. Use **Lifecycle Management** rules to archive blobs:

```json
{
  "rules": [
    {
      "enabled": true,
      "name": "archiveAfter30Days",
      "type": "Lifecycle",
      "definition": {
        "filters": { "blobTypes": ["blockBlob"] },
        "actions": {
          "baseBlob": {
            "tierToArchive": { "daysAfterModificationGreaterThan": 30
}
          }
        }
      }
    }
  ]
}
```

2. Delete unattached disks and snapshots:

```
az disk list --query "[?managedBy==null]" --output table
```

3. Move from Premium to Standard storage where performance permits.

4. Enable **Cool** or **Archive** tier for long-term logs, backups, or audit data.

Monitoring Utilization with Azure Monitor

Set up **dashboards and alerts** for:

- Underutilized resources

- Idle VMs

- Low network traffic on ExpressRoute

- High disk latency with low IOPS

- App Service plans with no recent activity

Use **Log Analytics** queries:

```
Perf
| where ObjectName == "Processor"
| summarize avg(CounterValue) by Computer
| where avg_CounterValue < 10
```

Re-architecting for Efficiency

In some cases, optimization requires architectural changes:

- **Monolith → Microservices**: Enables granular scaling

- **IaaS → PaaS**: Reduce management overhead and improve cost

- **PaaS → Serverless**: For high burst, low-average usage apps

- **SQL → Cosmos DB**: For globally distributed or scalable apps

- **Load balancers → Front Door/CDN**: Offload traffic and save bandwidth costs

Design services around consumption—not capacity.

Best Practices

- Review **Azure Advisor** weekly.

- Schedule **auto-shutdown** for non-production.

- Conduct **quarterly resource audits** with FinOps teams.

- Leverage **tagging** to track usage and accountability.

- Define **SLOs** to prevent over-engineering.

- Monitor with **budgets, alerts, and trend reports**.

- Use **Azure Policy** to enforce optimization (e.g., block high-SKU resources).

- Clean up orphaned resources post-deployment automatically with pipelines.

Conclusion

Optimization is not a one-time event—it's a continual practice that integrates monitoring, automation, architectural review, and accountability into the development lifecycle. With Azure's rich ecosystem of tools and services—from Advisor and Monitor to VM Scale Sets and lifecycle rules—architects have everything needed to tune resource usage precisely.

By rightsizing, automating, and shifting to modern compute and storage paradigms, you not only reduce spend but build leaner, faster, and more responsive cloud environments.

In the next section, we'll explore budgeting and alerting techniques to enforce financial accountability and prevent overspending across teams, departments, and projects.

Implementing Budgets and Alerts

Establishing financial control in cloud environments is a critical responsibility for architects, developers, and stakeholders alike. As cloud adoption grows across departments, teams, and workloads, ensuring that spending aligns with organizational goals becomes increasingly complex. That's where **budgets and alerts** come into play. Azure offers a range of native tools to define spending limits, trigger warnings, automate enforcement actions, and integrate financial governance into daily cloud operations.

This section explores the mechanisms available in Azure to define, monitor, and enforce budgets. It also provides practical examples, alert automation workflows, and governance strategies that can be implemented across different tiers of your organization—from projects and subscriptions to entire management groups.

Why Budgets and Alerts Matter

The elasticity of the cloud makes it easy to spin up resources and scale instantly. But without proactive financial controls, this can lead to:

- Budget   overruns

- Inconsistent   spend   tracking

- Unaccounted   shadow   IT   expenses

- Difficulty   in   chargebacks   and   showbacks

- Lack   of   stakeholder   visibility

Budgets and alerts help you:

- Define   **spending**   **thresholds**

- Notify   stakeholders   before   overruns

- Automate   responses   (e.g.,   shutdown   resources)

- Enforce   accountability   via   tagging   and   scopes

- Plan   more   accurately   for   future   expenses

Core Components

Azure provides the following features to implement budgets and alerts:

1. **Azure Budgets**: Define budget thresholds and track spend progress over time.

2. **Action Groups**: Trigger notifications or actions when a budget is breached.

3. **Cost Alerts**: Custom notifications based on actual or forecasted spend.

4. **Azure Policy**: Enforce governance to prevent resource misuse.

5. **Tags and Management Groups**: Scope budgets for departments, teams, or projects.

Creating a Budget in Azure

You can create budgets at the following scopes:

- Subscription

- Resource   group

- Management   group

- Billing   account

To create a budget via the Azure Portal:

1. Go   to   **Cost**   **Management**   +   **Billing**.

2. Choose   **Budgets**   →   Create.

3. Select   scope   (subscription,   resource   group,   etc.).

4. Set   budget   amount   (e.g., $2,000/month).

5. Define   time   period   (monthly,   quarterly,   annually).

6. Set   threshold   triggers   (e.g.,   80%,   90%,   100%).

Budgets support **actual spend** and **forecasted spend**.

Example: Create Budget via CLI

```
az consumption budget create \
  --amount 1000 \
```

```
--budget-name "DevTeamMonthlyBudget" \

--category cost \

--time-grain Monthly \

--start-date 2025-05-01 \

--end-date 2025-12-31 \

--time-period start=2025-05-01T00:00:00Z end=2025-12-31T23:59:59Z \

--resource-group myRG \

--notifications \

  actualGreaterThan=80% \

  thresholdType=Actual \

  contactEmails=devteam@example.com \

  contactRoles=Owner
```

This creates a monthly budget with email alerts at 80% usage.

Using Action Groups for Alerts

Action Groups define what happens when a threshold is reached. An action group can:

- Send an **email**
- Trigger a **webhook**
- Send SMS or push notifications
- Trigger a **Logic App**, **Function**, or **Automation Runbook**

Example: Create an Action Group with CLI

```
az monitor action-group create \

  --name CostAlertGroup \
```

```
--resource-group myRG \

--short-name alertgrp \

--action email admin admin@company.com
```

You can then attach this group to the budget or cost alert.

Forecast vs. Actual Budgets

Azure Budgets can evaluate both:

- **Actual usage**: Past consumption billed.

- **Forecast usage**: Projected usage based on current trend.

Use forecast-based budgets to **proactively mitigate** overruns.

Example: Alert when forecast exceeds budget

```
az consumption budget update \

  --budget-name DevBudget \

  --resource-group myRG \

  --notifications forecastedGreaterThan=90%
```

Using Cost Anomaly Detection

Azure Cost Management includes **Cost Anomaly Detection** for proactive alerting when a sudden cost increase is detected in usage patterns.

1. Go to **Cost Alerts**.

2. Enable anomaly detection for services, subscriptions, or resource groups.

3. Get notified when usage spikes beyond baseline deviation.

This is particularly useful for catching:

- Sudden   egress   spikes

- Misconfigured   auto-scaling

- Forgotten   test   environments

Scoping Budgets to Teams and Projects

Use **resource tags** and **management groups** to assign and monitor budgets per team or workload.

Tags:

```
az    tag    create    --resource-id    /subscriptions/<sub-
id>/resourceGroups/myRG --tags costcenter=marketing env=prod
```

Budgets can then be filtered to only resources matching certain tags, ensuring accurate showback and accountability.

For example:

- project: phoenix-app

- team: finance

- owner: jsmith

Management Groups allow budget creation across subscriptions with centralized visibility.

Budget Notifications and Enforcement

While budgets are non-enforcing by default, you can build **enforcement actions** using integrations:

- **Azure   Functions**   to   scale   down   resources

- **Logic   Apps**   to   trigger   approval   workflows

- **Automation** **Runbooks** to deallocate VMs
- **Policy** **Assignment** to prevent new high-cost SKUs

Example Function:

```python
import os

import azure.mgmt.compute

from azure.identity import DefaultAzureCredential


def main(req):

    vm_name = req.params.get('vm')

    resource_group = req.params.get('rg')

    compute_client                                          =
ComputeManagementClient(DefaultAzureCredential(),
os.environ["AZURE_SUBSCRIPTION_ID"])

    compute_client.virtual_machines.begin_deallocate(resource_group,
vm_name)
```

Trigger this via webhook from an Action Group when budget threshold hits 100%.

Reporting and Dashboards

Use **Azure Workbooks** or **Power BI** to create custom budget dashboards for leadership and finance.

Include:

- Budget vs. actual
- Forecast trends
- Cost by tag or department

- Alert history

- Growth rate over time

You can also schedule PDF exports or live links for transparency.

Best Practices

- Set **tiered thresholds** (e.g., 70%, 90%, 100%) with escalating actions.

- Combine **actual** + **forecasted alerts** for comprehensive coverage.

- Assign **clear ownership** for each budget.

- Track **unused budget capacity** to fund innovation.

- Review **alerts weekly** and refine thresholds over time.

- Use **shared Action Groups** to centralize alerting.

- Regularly audit **scope accuracy** (resource groups, tags, management groups).

- Integrate budget alerts into **incident response workflows**.

Real-World Example

An enterprise SaaS team with a $10,000 monthly budget:

- Budget 1: `project=saas-core`, $6,000, triggers alerts at 75%, 90%, 100%

- Budget 2: `project=saas-dev`, $2,000, stops test VMs at 90% via Logic App

- Budget 3: `project=saas-dataplatform`, $2,000, notifies CTO and triggers change review if forecasted spend hits 95%

All budgets are shown in a Power BI dashboard shared with finance, DevOps, and leadership weekly.

Conclusion

Budgets and alerts are essential components of financial governance in the cloud. When implemented thoughtfully, they provide guardrails for cloud usage, protect against surprise bills, and encourage accountability throughout your organization. By leveraging Azure Budgets, Action Groups, Cost Alerts, and integrations with automation tools, you can create a dynamic and responsive financial control framework that aligns spending with business priorities.

In the next chapter, we will shift our focus from financial operations to applied architecture, exploring real-world case studies and reusable patterns for building robust, scalable, and maintainable solutions on Azure.

Chapter 9: Case Studies and Architectural Patterns

Reference Architectures for Web Applications

Building modern web applications in Azure requires a careful blend of performance, scalability, resilience, security, and maintainability. Azure offers a robust platform to support full-stack development and deployment—from front-end hosting to backend services, databases, and global delivery via CDN and traffic management tools. In this section, we examine reference architectures for web applications across various complexity tiers, review common design decisions, and highlight real-world implementation strategies aligned with Azure best practices.

We'll explore scenarios ranging from small-scale apps to enterprise-grade SaaS platforms, covering architectural components, scalability options, deployment considerations, and monitoring strategies.

Foundational Concepts

A typical web application architecture consists of:

- **Frontend**: HTML/CSS/JavaScript code served to users via browsers

- **Backend API**: Handles business logic, authentication, and database access

- **Database**: Stores relational or NoSQL data

- **Cache**: Provides low-latency data retrieval

- **CI/CD Pipelines**: Automate deployments

- **Monitoring and Logging**: Observability tools for performance and error tracking

- **Security**: Identity, access controls, data protection

Azure provides all these building blocks in native PaaS offerings.

Small-Scale Web App Reference Architecture

Ideal for startups, MVPs, and internal tools.

Architecture Overview:

- **Azure App Service** (Web App)
- **Azure SQL Database** (Single DB)
- **Azure Blob Storage** (Media/static files)
- **Application Insights** (Monitoring)
- **GitHub Actions** (CI/CD)

Key Features:

- Cost-effective
- Simple to deploy and scale
- Limited customization required
- Use managed identity to connect securely to the database

CI/CD Workflow Example (GitHub Actions):

```
name: Deploy Web App

on:

  push:

    branches:

      - main

jobs:

  build-and-deploy:

    runs-on: ubuntu-latest

    steps:

      - uses: actions/checkout@v3

      - uses: azure/webapps-deploy@v2

        with:
```

```
app-name: myapp

publish-profile: ${{ secrets.AZURE_WEBAPP_PUBLISH_PROFILE
}}

package: .
```

Mid-Tier Architecture for Business Applications

For larger applications with increased traffic and team-based development.

Architecture Overview:

- **Azure App Service Plan** with Web App and Azure Functions
- **Azure API Management** (APIM)
- **Azure SQL Database** (vCore) or **Cosmos DB**
- **Azure Redis Cache**
- **Azure Key Vault** for secrets management
- **Azure Storage** for media
- **App Gateway** or **Front Door** for load balancing
- **Azure DevOps Pipelines**

Scalability:

- Use App Service autoscaling rules
- Use Redis to cache database calls
- Route requests via API Management for throttling and analytics

Security:

- Use Azure AD B2C or Azure AD for user auth
- Secure backend with private endpoints

- Implement NSGs and ASGs for network-level control

Monitoring:

- Application Insights for distributed tracing
- Azure Monitor logs for infrastructure health
- Log Analytics for queryable logs

Enterprise SaaS Application Reference Architecture

A robust, multi-tenant design supporting thousands of concurrent users across regions.

Architecture Overview:

- **Azure Kubernetes Service (AKS) or App Service Environment (ASE)**
- **Azure Cosmos DB (multi-region)**
- **Azure Front Door (global traffic routing and WAF)**
- **Azure API Management (Premium)**
- **Azure Key Vault with RBAC**
- **Azure Container Registry**
- **Azure Monitor and Log Analytics Workspace**
- **Azure DevOps or GitHub Enterprise for CI/CD**
- **Private DNS Zones, VNet Peering, and Private Link**

Multitenancy:

- Implement tenant isolation with database sharding or shared schemas
- Use B2B/B2C for identity federation
- Use feature flags for tenant-specific configurations

Global Delivery and Performance:

- Serve static assets via Azure CDN
- Geo-replicate databases
- Deploy AKS in multiple Azure regions and connect with Azure Traffic Manager

Security and Compliance:

- Use Managed Identity for access control
- Enable Defender for Cloud with regulatory compliance dashboard
- Enforce policy compliance with Azure Policy
- Encrypt data at rest and in transit

Common Web App Architectural Patterns

1. Backend for Frontend (BFF)

Custom API gateways that tailor responses for mobile, web, or third-party clients.

Azure Implementation:

- Use Azure API Management or Functions to create backend layers tailored to each client type.

2. CQRS (Command Query Responsibility Segregation)

Separate command and query operations for scalability.

Azure Implementation:

- Commands → Azure Functions with Service Bus
- Queries → Read-optimized Cosmos DB or SQL replicas

3. Micro Frontends

Split frontend codebase into independently deployed apps.

Azure Implementation:

- Deploy static frontend apps to different **App Services or Blob Storage** containers

- Aggregate via a reverse proxy or Web Component Shell

DevOps for Web Applications

Use infrastructure-as-code (IaC) and CI/CD for consistent, repeatable deployments.

IaC Options:

- **Bicep** or **ARM** **Templates**
- **Terraform** for multi-cloud portability

CI/CD Tools:

- **GitHub** **Actions**
- **Azure** **DevOps** **Pipelines**
- **ArgoCD** (if using AKS)

Pipeline Example with Azure DevOps:

```
trigger:

- main


pool:

  vmImage: 'ubuntu-latest'


steps:

- task: AzureWebApp@1

  inputs:

    azureSubscription: '<Service Connection>'
```

```
appName: 'myWebApp'

package: '$(System.DefaultWorkingDirectory)/drop.zip'
```

Include steps for:

- Linting

- Testing

- Build

- Deploy

- Health   check   verification

- Rollback   logic

Monitoring and Troubleshooting

Instrument web apps with:

- **Application Insights**: Request   metrics,   performance,   failures,   availability

- **Log   Analytics**:   KQL   queries   across   logs

- **Azure Monitor Alerts**: Trigger   alerts   on   CPU,   error   count,   latency

- **Azure Workbooks**:   Dashboards   for   product   and   dev   teams

Sample KQL Query:

```
requests

| where timestamp > ago(24h)

| summarize count() by resultCode, url
```

Recommendations

- Start simple (App Service + SQL) and evolve toward complex (AKS + APIM + Cosmos) as needed.

- Use CDN and caching layers to improve performance and reduce backend load.

- Protect apps with WAF (Web Application Firewall) via Azure Front Door or App Gateway.

- Use managed identities to access secrets, storage, and databases.

- Tag and organize resources by environment, app, and owner for visibility.

Conclusion

Whether you're building a startup MVP or an enterprise SaaS platform, Azure provides the flexibility and depth to support modern web architectures at every scale. By choosing the right reference architecture, incorporating automation, and layering in security and observability, you set the foundation for high-performance, resilient, and cost-effective applications.

In the next section, we'll explore reusable integration patterns, including messaging, APIs, and hybrid cloud designs that enable complex enterprise applications to thrive in Azure.

Patterns for Enterprise Integration

Enterprise applications rarely exist in isolation. Whether integrating legacy systems, SaaS platforms, internal microservices, or partner APIs, seamless **integration** is the lifeblood of modern digital ecosystems. In the Azure ecosystem, Microsoft provides a wide range of services and architectural patterns that enable reliable, scalable, and maintainable integrations across diverse systems.

This section delves into core patterns for enterprise integration using Azure services. We'll explore message-based communication, API gateway strategies, event-driven designs, hybrid connectivity, workflow orchestration, and real-world implementation tactics. Each pattern serves a distinct purpose, from decoupling and reliability to observability and transformation.

Key Integration Challenges in Enterprises

- **System heterogeneity** (mainframes, on-prem, cloud-native apps)

- **Asynchronous processing** (due to network, batch jobs, and SLAs)

- **Security and compliance** (data sovereignty, encryption)

- **Scalability** (bursty loads, unpredictable demand)

- **Data consistency and duplication** (eventual consistency)

- **Change management** (adding/changing endpoints without disruption)

These challenges necessitate **design patterns** that abstract complexity while promoting agility and robustness.

Pattern 1: Messaging Queue-Based Integration

Scenario: Decouple systems by introducing message queues that act as buffers between producer and consumer services.

Azure Services:

- **Azure Service Bus** (enterprise-grade)

- **Azure Queue Storage** (lightweight, simple)

Benefits:

- Decouples systems (loose coupling)

- Enables retries and dead-lettering

- Provides durability and resiliency

- Supports message ordering and sessions

Implementation Tips:

- Use **topics** for fan-out scenarios

- Set up **dead-letter queues** for failed processing

- Implement **peek-lock** mechanism to avoid message loss

- Use **managed identities** for secure access

Example configuration for Service Bus queue using Azure CLI:

```
az servicebus queue create \
```

```
--resource-group myRG \

--namespace-name myNamespace \

--name myQueue \

--enable-dead-lettering-on-message-expiration true
```

Use Azure Functions or Logic Apps to subscribe to queue messages and process them asynchronously.

Pattern 2: API Gateway Pattern

Scenario: Front multiple backend services with a unified API surface.

Azure Services:

- **Azure   API   Management   (APIM)**

Benefits:

- Centralized   authentication,   throttling,   and   logging
- Enables   versioning   and   developer   portals
- Supports   transformations   and   request   rewriting
- Facilitates   secure   third-party   access

Common Use Cases:

- Partner   integration   APIs
- Public   and   private   product   APIs
- Mobile   backend   for   frontend   (BFF)   designs

Design Considerations:

- Create   products   in   APIM   to   group   APIs   and   control   access

- Use policies for transformations (XML to JSON, schema enforcement)
- Enable **OAuth2**, **JWT** **validation**, or **subscription** **key** **access**
- Set up **rate** **limiting** **and** **quotas**

Example policy to validate JWT:

```
<validate-jwt header-name="Authorization" failed-validation-httpcode="401" failed-validation-error-message="Unauthorized">

    <openid-config
url="https://login.microsoftonline.com/{tenant}/v2.0/.well-known/openid-configuration" />

    <required-claims>

        <claim name="aud">

            <value>api://my-api-id</value>

        </claim>

    </required-claims>

</validate-jwt>
```

Pattern 3: Event-Driven Integration

Scenario: React to changes across systems in near real-time via events instead of polling.

Azure Services:

- **Azure** **Event** **Grid**
- **Azure** **Event** **Hubs** (high-volume telemetry)
- **Azure** **Service** **Bus** **Topics** (ordered events)
- **Azure** **Functions**, **Logic** **Apps** for subscribers

Benefits:

- Real-time processing
- Lightweight event schema
- Scalable fan-out
- Supports custom and system topics

Use Cases:

- Notify downstream services when a file is uploaded
- Trigger workflows when a database update occurs
- Send alerts based on event patterns

Best Practices:

- Use **event schemas** (CloudEvents 1.0)
- Use **dead-lettering** and **retry policies**
- Avoid duplicate events by tracking IDs or using deduplication

---

Pattern 4: Hybrid Integration with On-Prem Systems

Scenario: Integrate Azure services with legacy or on-prem systems that are not cloud-ready.

Azure Services:

- **Azure ExpressRoute** or **VPN Gateway** for private network connectivity
- **Azure Arc** for hybrid management
- **On-Prem Data Gateway** (for Logic Apps, Power BI, Power Automate)
- **Azure Relay** for firewall-friendly communication

Use Cases:

- Connect on-prem SQL Server to Azure Data Factory

- Expose on-prem APIs to Azure Apps without opening firewall ports

- Run hybrid workloads like SAP, Oracle, IBM MQ

Security Tips:

- Use **Private** **Link** where supported

- Employ **NSGs** **and** **firewalls** on the Azure side

- Use **Hybrid** **Identity** for consistent access controls

Pattern 5: Workflow Orchestration

Scenario: Define end-to-end business processes that coordinate across APIs, queues, and data services.

Azure Services:

- **Logic** **Apps** (low-code)

- **Durable** **Functions** (code-first)

- **Azure** **Data** **Factory** (data-centric workflows)

Benefits:

- Built-in connectors to hundreds of systems

- Visual designer for workflows

- Retry, timeout, and compensation support

- Long-running stateful orchestration with Durable Functions

Example Workflow:

1. Receive an order from API

2. Store metadata in Cosmos DB

3. Send a message to Service Bus

4. Wait for warehouse acknowledgment

5. Send confirmation email to customer

Use **chaining**, **fan-out/fan-in**, and **human approval** steps.

Pattern 6: File-Based Integration

Scenario: Exchange data between systems via files (CSV, XML, JSON).

Azure Services:

- **Azure Blob Storage**
- **Azure Data Factory**
- **Azure Logic Apps**
- **Event Grid on Blob Events**

Common Use Cases:

- Daily batch imports or exports
- Legacy ERP integration
- File drops into secure container

Recommendations:

- Enable **blob versioning and soft delete**
- Trigger downstream workflows via **Event Grid**
- Use **SAS tokens** or **managed identities** for secure access

---

Security and Compliance in Integration

Every integration point is a potential security risk. Implement:

- **API gateways** for exposure control
- **Managed identities** for secure service-to-service access
- **Role-based access control (RBAC)** across resources
- **Key Vault** for managing secrets and credentials
- **Logging and tracing** for every transaction path
- **Azure Policy** to enforce standards (e.g., TLS enforcement, regional restrictions)

Use **Azure Sentinel** or **Microsoft Defender for Cloud** to monitor threats across integration surfaces.

Monitoring and Observability

To maintain visibility across complex integrations:

- Use **Azure Monitor** to collect logs and metrics from APIs, queues, services
- Use **Application Insights** for end-to-end tracing
- Use **Log Analytics** to correlate logs

Example KQL query:

```
AzureDiagnostics

| where ResourceType == "AZUREAPIMANAGEMENT"

| summarize count() by OperationName_s, StatusCode_s, bin(TimeGenerated, 1h)
```

Best Practices

- Favor asynchronous messaging to decouple producers and consumers.
- Use API gateways to standardize access and secure external interfaces.

- Prefer event-driven models where real-time response is required.

- Use retry logic and idempotent operations to handle failures gracefully.

- Secure every component with RBAC and Private Endpoints.

- Automate deployment of integration components using Bicep, ARM, or Terraform.

- Continuously test integration workflows with mock endpoints and data.

Conclusion

Enterprise integration is no longer a side concern—it's a core architectural function. With Azure's extensive suite of integration services and patterns, you can unify legacy systems, SaaS platforms, microservices, and data pipelines into cohesive, intelligent ecosystems.

By choosing the right pattern for the job—be it messaging, APIs, events, or workflows—you not only build resilient and scalable systems but also future-proof your enterprise for innovation and growth.

In the next section, we'll dive into hybrid cloud architectures and examine how to connect Azure with on-premises environments for seamless operational continuity and data sharing.

Hybrid Cloud and On-Prem Integration

For many enterprises, full migration to the cloud is not immediately feasible or strategically desirable. Existing investments in on-premises infrastructure, regulatory requirements, data sovereignty concerns, and performance dependencies often require a **hybrid cloud architecture**. Azure offers a comprehensive suite of tools and services to seamlessly connect on-premises data centers with Azure's global cloud infrastructure, enabling organizations to modernize their workloads incrementally and securely.

This section explores the key architectural considerations, tools, patterns, and real-world practices for building robust hybrid solutions with Azure. We'll examine connectivity, identity, data integration, management, and governance strategies that bridge the gap between on-prem and cloud environments.

The Need for Hybrid Architectures

Hybrid cloud enables businesses to:

- **Extend existing infrastructure** to the cloud without disrupting services

- **Maintain compliance** with industry-specific regulations (e.g., GDPR, HIPAA, PCI-DSS)

- **Enable gradual cloud adoption** via phased migrations

- **Support edge computing** for latency-sensitive applications

- **Unify management and operations** across environments

Hybrid strategies are particularly useful in industries such as healthcare, finance, government, and manufacturing, where strict governance and data locality are crucial.

Core Hybrid Integration Scenarios

1. **Network   Connectivity**

   ○ Secure, performant, and scalable network paths between on-prem and Azure

2. **Identity   Federation**

   ○ Unified identity and access management across environments

3. **Data   Synchronization   and   Replication**

   ○ Consistent access to critical data across systems

4. **Application   Integration**

   ○ Hybrid APIs, workflows, and message brokering

5. **Unified   Management   and   Governance**

   ○ Central monitoring, policy, and automation

Networking for Hybrid Cloud

Azure ExpressRoute

A private, high-throughput connection from on-prem to Azure.

- Avoids   the   public   internet

- Offers predictable latency and higher reliability
- Available in metered and unlimited data plans

Use Cases:

- Mission-critical data transfers
- Compliance-heavy workloads
- Low-latency requirements (SAP, databases)

Setup:

1. Partner with ExpressRoute provider
2. Configure ExpressRoute Circuit in Azure
3. Link to a Virtual Network Gateway

```
az network express-route create \
  --name myER \
  --resource-group myRG \
  --location eastus \
  --bandwidth 200 \
  --provider "Equinix" \
  --peering-location "Silicon Valley" \
  --sku-family MeteredData \
  --sku-tier Standard
```

Azure VPN Gateway

Site-to-site or point-to-site encrypted tunnels over the public internet.

- Ideal for lightweight and dev/test connectivity

- IPsec/IKE protocol support

```
az network vpn-gateway create \
  --name myVPN \
  --resource-group myRG \
  --vnet myVNet \
  --public-ip-address myPublicIP
```

Virtual WAN

Azure's managed hub-and-spoke architecture for large-scale hybrid networks.

- Simplifies connection to multiple branches, regions, and users
- Supports SD-WAN integration

Hybrid Identity and Access Management

Azure AD provides identity federation between on-prem AD and Azure-based services.

Azure AD Connect

Synchronizes identities from on-prem AD to Azure AD.

- Supports password hash sync or pass-through authentication
- Enables Single Sign-On (SSO)
- Supports hybrid join for devices

Best Practices:

- Use **staging mode** for backup sync server
- Implement **Azure Conditional Access**
- Integrate with **Privileged Identity Management (PIM)**

Azure AD Domain Services

Provides domain-join, group policy, and LDAP compatibility in Azure without managing DCs.

- Supports legacy apps needing AD

- Ideal for lift-and-shift migrations

Data Integration Between On-Prem and Azure

Azure Data Factory

Hybrid ETL/ELT service for moving data between cloud and on-prem systems.

- Supports on-prem SQL, Oracle, SAP, Teradata, and file shares

- Use Self-hosted Integration Runtime (IR) to connect securely

```
az datafactory integration-runtime self-hosted create \

  --resource-group myRG \

  --factory-name myDF \

  --name selfhostedIR
```

Azure File Sync

Syncs on-prem file servers with Azure Files.

- Keeps frequently accessed files local

- Tier older data to cloud

- Centralize file share backups

Use Cases:

- Branch office file servers

- Disaster recovery of NAS systems

SQL Server Stretch Database

Allows dynamic offloading of cold data from on-prem SQL Server to Azure SQL Database.

- Keeps active data on-prem for performance
- Moves older rows to Azure seamlessly

Application and Message Integration

Azure Relay

Enables apps to securely expose services over firewalls/NAT without public IPs.

- Ideal for hybrid WCF apps and APIs
- Uses WebSockets and hybrid connections

Azure Logic Apps + On-Prem Data Gateway

Connect Azure Logic Apps to on-prem services (SQL Server, SAP, Oracle, etc.)

Setup:

1. Install on-prem gateway agent
2. Register with Azure
3. Use Logic App connectors referencing the gateway

Azure Service Bus and Event Grid

- Use **Service Bus** for reliable messaging between on-prem and cloud systems
- Use **Event Grid** to trigger Azure workflows on file drops, DB updates, etc.

Hybrid Application Hosting

Azure Stack HCI / Azure Stack Hub

- Run Azure services on-prem in disconnected or regulated environments

- Extend Azure VMs, Kubernetes, and PaaS workloads locally

Container and Kubernetes Integration

- Use **Azure Arc** to manage on-prem Kubernetes clusters
- Deploy apps from Azure DevOps to on-prem clusters using GitOps

```
az connectedk8s connect --name myOnPremK8s --resource-group myRG
```

Unified Monitoring and Management

Use **Azure Monitor**, **Log Analytics**, and **Azure Arc** for unified visibility.

Monitor On-Prem Resources:

- Deploy **Log Analytics Agent**
- Collect logs, metrics, and alerts
- Integrate with **Azure Sentinel** for security insights

Governance Tools:

- **Azure Policy** with Arc-enabled resources
- **Azure Blueprints** for hybrid compliance baselines
- **Azure Lighthouse** for MSPs to manage hybrid clients

Security Considerations

- Use **Private Link** to connect services without public exposure
- Implement **Just-in-Time (JIT)** VM access
- Encrypt all data in transit and at rest (TLS 1.2+, Azure-managed keys or CMKs)

- Maintain identity governance using **Azure AD PIM** and **Conditional Access**

Real-World Use Case: Manufacturing Firm

Scenario: A global manufacturing company runs ERP systems on-prem and is adopting Azure for predictive maintenance analytics.

Architecture:

- On-prem PLCs stream telemetry to **local edge gateways**
- Data flows via **ExpressRoute** into Azure IoT Hub
- **Azure Stream Analytics** performs real-time processing
- Maintenance results stored in **Azure SQL**
- Workers access dashboards via **Power BI**
- AD accounts federated via **Azure AD Connect**

Outcomes:

- 20% reduction in machine downtime
- Secure, compliant data handling
- Hybrid governance across all systems

Best Practices

- Start with **network and identity foundation**
- Tag hybrid resources for visibility and cost management
- Use **ExpressRoute for critical data**, VPN for non-critical
- Monitor everything centrally with Azure Monitor and Sentinel
- Automate integration flows using Logic Apps and Data Factory

- Audit and rotate credentials frequently

- Define RTO/RPO requirements across hybrid boundaries

Conclusion

Hybrid cloud isn't a compromise—it's a strategic enabler. With Azure's comprehensive hybrid toolset, enterprises can modernize their infrastructure at their own pace, maintain compliance, and extend innovation beyond data center walls. Whether you're bridging legacy systems, deploying at the edge, or operating in highly regulated environments, Azure offers the flexibility and control to build a truly hybrid architecture that evolves with your needs.

In the next section, we'll explore key insights from real-world deployments—highlighting lessons learned, common pitfalls, and architectural decisions that separate successful cloud projects from those that fail to deliver on their promise.

Lessons from Real-World Deployments

Designing and deploying cloud architecture is not just about choosing the right services—it's about applying them effectively in dynamic, real-world environments. Despite meticulous planning, many projects experience unexpected complexities, ranging from scaling issues to misaligned stakeholder expectations. Conversely, successful deployments tend to share certain key traits: iterative delivery, cross-team collaboration, rigorous cost monitoring, and a strong DevOps culture.

This section synthesizes lessons learned from real Azure implementations across industries including finance, healthcare, e-commerce, and manufacturing. Through these insights, architects and engineers can avoid common pitfalls, adopt proven best practices, and build scalable, secure, and sustainable solutions.

Lesson 1: Start with Clear Business Goals

Case: A fintech startup over-engineered its Azure Kubernetes Service (AKS) deployment, investing weeks in setting up CI/CD, custom ingress controllers, and multi-tenant separation. However, their actual business need was to support a beta MVP for investor demos.

Lesson:

- Always align architectural decisions with business goals and timelines.

- Complexity should match current stage, not imagined scale.

Best Practice:

- Begin with **App Services** or **Container Apps** for MVPs.

- Migrate to AKS or other advanced services as needs grow.

Lesson 2: Design for Observability from Day One

Case: A healthcare company faced outages in production after deploying a new API backend. There were no structured logs, tracing, or metrics, leading to a 3-day root cause investigation.

Lesson:

- Observability isn't a nice-to-have—it's essential.

- Retrofitting monitoring is harder than building it in from the start.

Best Practice:

- Implement **Azure Monitor**, **Application Insights**, and **Log Analytics** as foundational layers.

- Define service-level indicators (SLIs) and objectives (SLOs).

- Use **Workbooks** and **dashboards** for shared visibility.

Lesson 3: Overprovisioning Happens—Optimize Early

Case: An e-commerce platform launched with App Service Premium plans across all environments. By the end of year one, 65% of their monthly spend was on unused capacity.

Lesson:

- Defaulting to premium SKUs may ensure performance—but often wastes money.

Best Practice:

- Start with minimal viable infrastructure.

- Use **Azure Advisor** to review performance and scale gradually.

- Employ **Auto-scale rules** and **scheduled shutdowns** for dev/test workloads.

Lesson 4: Use Infrastructure as Code Consistently

Case: A multinational used manual resource creation in production due to time pressure. Later, they faced environment drift and errors during disaster recovery.

Lesson:

- Manual configurations are fragile and hard to reproduce.

Best Practice:

- Standardize on **Terraform,** **Bicep,** or **ARM** **templates**.
- Version-control all infrastructure definitions.
- Include environment promotion (dev → staging → prod) in CI/CD pipelines.

Example Terraform snippet for tagging consistency:

```
resource "azurerm_resource_group" "example" {

  name      = "example-rg"

  location = "eastus"

  tags = {

    environment = "production"

    owner       = "infra-team"

  }

}
```

Lesson 5: Authentication and Authorization Require Planning

Case: A retail company enabled public APIs quickly without configuring proper identity management. After going live, they experienced unauthorized data exposure.

Lesson:

- Security must be foundational, not an afterthought.

Best Practice:

- Use **Azure AD**, **B2C**, or **MSAL** SDKs for app authentication.

- Secure APIs with **API Management** **policies** and **OAuth2**.

- Use **Key Vault** to manage secrets and connection strings.

- Regularly audit access controls and RBAC assignments.

Lesson 6: Avoid "Lift and Shift" Without Refactoring

Case: A logistics company moved 20 on-prem VMs to Azure via rehosting but failed to optimize configurations. Costs increased 45% and app latency worsened.

Lesson:

- Cloud-native benefits require **cloud-native design**.

Best Practice:

- Rehost only for short-term continuity.

- Evaluate apps for **PaaS refactoring** or **containerization**.

- Use **Azure Migrate** for right-sizing and dependency analysis.

Lesson 7: Build for Failure—Always

Case: A SaaS provider used only one region for all services. A regional outage caused complete downtime for customers and delayed SLA responses.

Lesson:

- Regional redundancy and failure planning are not optional.

Best Practice:

- Use **Availability Zones** for intra-region HA.
- Use **Azure Traffic Manager** or **Front Door** for geo-redundancy.
- Regularly test **disaster recovery (DR)** plans.
- Design with **circuit breakers** and **retries** in microservices.

Lesson 8: Embrace DevOps Culture Early

Case: A media company siloed its infrastructure and development teams. Configuration changes took days, leading to missed deadlines and growing tech debt.

Lesson:

- DevOps is as much about culture as tools.

Best Practice:

- Foster cross-functional teams with shared ownership.
- Use tools like **Azure DevOps**, **GitHub Actions**, and **Boards**.
- Automate testing, linting, security scanning, and deployments.

Example Azure DevOps CI/CD stages:

```
stages:
  - stage: Build
    jobs:
      - job: BuildApp
        steps:
          - task: DotNetCoreCLI@2
```

```
    inputs:

      command: build

      projects: '**/*.csproj'
- stage: Deploy

  jobs:

    - job: DeployToDev

      steps:

        - task: AzureWebApp@1

          inputs:

            azureSubscription: 'MyServiceConnection'

            appName: 'myApp'

            package: '$(Build.ArtifactStagingDirectory)/drop.zip'
```

Lesson 9: Monitor and Review Costs Monthly

Case: A nonprofit received Azure credits but had no cost alerts. Within three months, 80% of the credits were consumed due to rogue services and forgotten test environments.

Lesson:

- Cost visibility must be ongoing and democratized.

Best Practice:

- Set **budgets** **and** **alerts** for every subscription.
- Review **Cost** **Management** **+** **Billing** monthly.
- Implement **tagging** **strategies** for accountability.
- Integrate **Power** **BI** **dashboards** for non-technical stakeholders.

Lesson 10: Document and Share Knowledge

Case: A transportation firm struggled with onboarding new engineers because tribal knowledge was stored in individual notebooks and outdated Confluence pages.

Lesson:

- Documentation is a multiplier for team productivity.

Best Practice:

- Maintain versioned **README files**, **architecture diagrams**, and **runbooks**.

- Use **Azure Wiki**, **Notion**, or **SharePoint** with markdown support.

- Record **decision logs (ADRs)** for architecture choices.

Conclusion

Real-world Azure deployments teach us that technical expertise alone isn't enough. The best outcomes stem from strategic alignment, continuous optimization, strong security hygiene, clear ownership, and tight feedback loops between people and systems.

These lessons are not one-size-fits-all, but when adapted to your organization's goals and maturity, they provide a practical compass for navigating the challenges of cloud adoption and evolution.

In the next chapter, we'll explore future-facing trends in cloud architecture—ranging from serverless and edge computing to Azure-integrated AI and quantum services—that are shaping the next generation of distributed, intelligent applications.

Chapter 10: The Future of Cloud Architecture on Azure

Azure AI and Machine Learning Integration

Artificial Intelligence (AI) and Machine Learning (ML) are no longer futuristic concepts reserved for research labs. Today, they are vital components of enterprise strategies for automation, analytics, and innovation. Microsoft Azure offers a mature, production-grade ecosystem for building, deploying, and scaling AI/ML workloads that can be embedded directly into applications and infrastructure.

As cloud-native architecture evolves, intelligent systems are becoming first-class citizens. Azure's AI services empower organizations to automate complex decision-making, personalize user experiences, detect anomalies, and gain deep insights from data—faster and more accurately than ever before.

This section explores the tools, patterns, and architectural models available in Azure for AI/ML integration, covering both custom model development and prebuilt services.

Azure AI and ML Ecosystem Overview

Azure provides a layered set of tools and services to accommodate the full spectrum of AI maturity—from beginner-level solutions to deep customization and scalability for data scientists.

Categories:

- **Azure AI Services**: Prebuilt, ready-to-use APIs (Vision, Language, Search, etc.)

- **Azure Machine Learning (Azure ML)**: Comprehensive ML platform for model building, training, deployment

- **Azure OpenAI Service**: Access to GPT models for natural language use cases

- **Cognitive Search**: AI-powered enterprise search

- **AI Infrastructure**: GPU VMs, Kubernetes, and hybrid ML deployment

Prebuilt Azure AI Services

Azure AI Services are RESTful APIs backed by state-of-the-art AI models, allowing developers to quickly infuse intelligence into applications without training their own models.

Categories & Use Cases:

- **Vision**:
  - Image classification, OCR, face detection, spatial analysis
- **Language**:
  - Sentiment analysis, language detection, named entity recognition, translation
- **Speech**:
  - Speech-to-text, text-to-speech, speaker recognition
- **Decision**:
  - Personalizer, Content Moderator, Anomaly Detector

Example: Sentiment Analysis (Text Analytics API)

```
POST
https://<region>.api.cognitive.microsoft.com/text/analytics/v3.0/sen
timent

Ocp-Apim-Subscription-Key: <your-key>

Content-Type: application/json


{

  "documents": [

    {

      "language": "en",

      "id": "1",

      "text": "The product launch was amazing!"

    }
```

```
  ]

}
```

Response:

```
{

  "documents": [

    {

      "id": "1",

      "sentiment": "positive",

      "confidenceScores": {

        "positive": 0.98,

        "neutral": 0.01,

        "negative": 0.01

      }

    }

  ]

}
```

These services are accessible via SDKs or REST, require minimal setup, and can be scaled instantly.

Azure Machine Learning (Azure ML)

Azure ML is a fully managed platform for:

- Data   preparation

- Model   training   and   tuning

- Deployment and MLOps
- Responsible AI and governance

Key Features:

- **Workspaces** for experiment tracking
- **Compute clusters** with auto-scaling
- **Model registry** and deployment endpoints
- **Pipeline orchestration** with ML pipelines
- **Notebooks, CLI, SDK,** and **drag-and-drop Designer**

Architecture:

1. **Ingest and prepare data** from Azure Blob, SQL, or external sources
2. **Train model** on scalable compute (CPU/GPU)
3. **Track experiments** with metrics, logs, versions
4. **Deploy as REST endpoint** or containerized microservice
5. **Monitor drift** and retrain with Azure Data Factory or Logic Apps

---

MLOps on Azure

MLOps brings DevOps principles to AI/ML projects, enabling repeatability, automation, and monitoring.

Tools & Services:

- Azure ML Pipelines (CI/CD for ML)
- Azure DevOps or GitHub Actions integration
- Azure Container Registry for model packaging
- Azure Key Vault for credential handling

- Application Insights for telemetry

Best Practices:

- Store training code in Git
- Automate pipeline triggers based on data updates
- Use **model versioning** and shadow deployments
- Audit and log all predictions for compliance

Example GitHub Action for training model:

```
jobs:

  train-model:

    runs-on: ubuntu-latest

    steps:

    - uses: actions/checkout@v3

    - name: Train model on Azure ML

      run: az ml job create --file job.yml --resource-group myRG --
workspace-name myWS
```

Azure OpenAI Service

Azure OpenAI provides access to advanced **language models** like GPT-4, Codex, and DALL·E through the Azure ecosystem, combining Microsoft's compliance and scalability with OpenAI's research.

Use Cases:

- Chatbots and virtual assistants
- Code generation and refactoring
- Document summarization and Q&A

- Natural language to SQL queries
- Content generation (ads, reports)

Security Benefits:

- Enterprise-grade identity and access
- Region control
- Private endpoint support
- Usage quotas and logging

Example prompt interaction (via SDK):

```
from openai import AzureOpenAI


client = AzureOpenAI(

    api_key="YOUR_API_KEY",

    api_version="2024-03-01-preview",

    azure_endpoint="https://your-openai-resource.openai.azure.com"

)


response = client.chat.completions.create(

    model="gpt-4",

    messages=[

        {"role": "system", "content": "You are an Azure architecture assistant."},

        {"role": "user", "content": "Explain Azure Front Door in simple terms."}

    ]
```

)

```
print(response.choices[0].message.content)
```

Cognitive Search + AI Enrichment

Azure **Cognitive Search** offers semantic search, text extraction, OCR, and metadata enrichment powered by AI.

Architecture:

1. Ingest documents (PDFs, DOCX, etc.)
2. Use AI enrichment pipeline (e.g., OCR, entity recognition)
3. Index results for search
4. Expose via API or integrated frontend

Use Cases:

- Legal or healthcare document search
- Support knowledge bases
- E-discovery and compliance
- Intelligent document processing (IDP)

Responsible AI and Governance

Responsible AI in Azure is supported by:

- **Fairness, transparency, and explainability** tooling
- **Model interpretability** via SHAP, LIME
- **Data privacy** protections (differential privacy, masking)

- **Audit trails** and lineage tracking
- **Security** with role-based access, network isolation, and encryption

Governance Tools:

- Azure Purview for data cataloging
- Azure Policy for data access control
- Azure Monitor for audit trails

Hybrid and Edge AI

Azure extends AI to the edge with:

- **Azure Percept** and **Azure IoT Edge**
- **ONNX Runtime** for optimized models
- **Custom Vision** for camera-based applications
- **Azure Stack Edge** for local inferencing

Use Cases:

- Real-time quality control on factory lines
- Video surveillance analytics
- Predictive maintenance for machinery
- Retail shelf and footfall analysis

Integration with Cloud-Native Apps

Embedding AI in existing Azure-native architecture:

- **Azure Functions** to trigger AI predictions

- **Event Grid** to react to model outputs
- **API Management** to expose ML endpoints
- **Logic Apps** for low-code orchestration

Example Use Case:

- User uploads a document to Blob Storage
- Event Grid triggers Logic App
- Logic App calls Cognitive Services for OCR and language detection
- Extracted text stored in Cosmos DB

Best Practices for AI/ML in Azure

- Start with **prebuilt AI services** to accelerate delivery
- Use **Azure ML** for advanced customization and control
- Monitor deployed models with telemetry and drift detection
- Secure AI endpoints with **Managed Identity** and **VNET integration**
- Leverage **AutoML** when data science resources are limited
- Track **experiment metadata** and maintain **model lineage**

Conclusion

Azure's AI and Machine Learning capabilities empower developers, data scientists, and enterprises to build smarter applications that learn, adapt, and deliver measurable impact. Whether integrating prebuilt APIs or training custom models, Azure offers the tools, infrastructure, and governance features required for scalable, ethical, and secure AI adoption.

In the next section, we'll explore the rise of serverless computing, how it reshapes application design, and what role it plays in creating cost-efficient, event-driven, and resilient architectures in Azure.

Serverless Computing Trends

Serverless computing has become a cornerstone of modern cloud-native architecture. It enables developers to build and deploy applications without worrying about infrastructure provisioning, maintenance, or scaling. Azure's serverless platform, including **Azure Functions**, **Azure Logic Apps**, **Event Grid**, and **Container Apps**, continues to evolve, offering more flexibility, integrations, and cost efficiency than ever before.

In this section, we explore the current and future trends of serverless computing in Azure, examining architectural patterns, service capabilities, real-world use cases, operational best practices, and how organizations can fully embrace event-driven and microservices paradigms. The shift from traditional server-based models to event-based, stateless execution environments is not just a trend—it's a long-term transformation that's reshaping application development at its core.

What is Serverless?

Serverless computing abstracts away the concept of servers entirely. It allows developers to write code that is automatically triggered by events, runs in ephemeral containers, and scales dynamically without explicit infrastructure management.

Key Characteristics:

- No infrastructure provisioning or server management

- Built-in auto-scaling and concurrency management

- Event-driven execution

- Billing based on actual usage (CPU/Memory/Execution Time)

Key Azure Serverless Services

1. **Azure Functions** – Run backend code in response to events or HTTP requests

2. **Azure Logic Apps** – Design low-code workflows for automation and integration

3. **Azure Event Grid** – Manage events across services and domains

4. **Azure Container Apps** – Serverless containers with scaling and microservices support

5. **Azure API Management** – Publish and secure serverless APIs

6. **Azure Durable Functions** – Build complex orchestrations and stateful workflows

---

Trend 1: Convergence of Serverless and Microservices

While serverless functions are inherently stateless and ephemeral, organizations are increasingly using them as **microservices**—smaller, independent components that focus on specific business logic.

Advantages:

- Faster development and deployment cycles
- Fine-grained scaling per function/microservice
- Independent fault domains
- Clear ownership and lifecycle boundaries

Pattern:

- Use **Azure Functions** for business logic
- **API Management** to expose as RESTful endpoints
- **Azure Cosmos DB** or **Table Storage** for persistence
- **Event Grid** to connect between services

Example:

- CreateUser function → triggers SendWelcomeEmail
- OrderPlaced event → triggers InventoryUpdate function
- Stateless services, orchestrated asynchronously

Trend 2: Event-Driven Architectures

Serverless thrives in **event-driven** systems. Events such as file uploads, database updates, HTTP requests, IoT telemetry, and business transactions can trigger serverless workflows.

Common Event Sources:

- Blob   Storage

- Cosmos   DB   change   feed

- Event   Grid   custom   topics

- Service   Bus   queues   and   topics

- HTTP   APIs   and   Webhooks

Benefits:

- Decoupled   producers   and   consumers

- High   responsiveness   and   scalability

- Near   real-time   processing

Example: Blob Storage Trigger in Azure Function

```
[FunctionName("ProcessUploadedFile")]

public void Run(

    [BlobTrigger("uploads/{name}",            Connection       =
"AzureWebJobsStorage")] Stream inputBlob,

    string name, ILogger log)

{

    log.LogInformation($"Processing blob: {name}");

    // Processing logic here

}
```

Trend 3: Serverless Containers

Azure Container Apps offer the flexibility of containers with serverless execution. Unlike Azure Functions, they support:

- Long-running   workloads

- Custom   runtimes   and   dependencies

- Background   processing

- HTTP   and   gRPC

Use Cases:

- Containerized   APIs   with   dynamic   scaling

- Real-time   stream   processing   (e.g.,   Dapr   +   KEDA)

- ML   inferencing   workloads

Features:

- Scale   to   zero   (and   back)   using   KEDA   triggers

- Dapr   integration   for   service   discovery   and   state   management

- GitHub   Actions   integration   for   deployments

Example deployment with Bicep:

```
resource containerApp 'Microsoft.App/containerApps@2022-03-01' = {

  name: 'myapp'

  location: resourceGroup().location

  properties: {

    configuration: {

      ingress: {

        external: true

        targetPort: 80

      }
```

```
  }

  template: {

    containers: [

      {

        name: 'appcontainer'

        image: 'myregistry.azurecr.io/myapp:latest'

      }

    ]

  }

}

}
```

Trend 4: Complex Orchestrations with Durable Functions

Azure **Durable Functions** add state and coordination to serverless logic through function chaining, fan-out/fan-in, and human interaction patterns.

Orchestration Patterns:

- Sequential   function   execution

- Parallel   processing   with   aggregation

- External   event   listeners

- Timers   and   delays

Use Case Example:

- Order   processing   workflow:

    - Validate   inventory

- ○ Process payment
- ○ Send confirmation email
- ○ Wait for delivery acknowledgment

Durable Function Example (Orchestrator):

```
[FunctionName("OrderProcessing")]

public static async Task Run(

    [OrchestrationTrigger] IDurableOrchestrationContext context)

{

    var order = context.GetInput<Order>();

    await context.CallActivityAsync("ValidateInventory", order);

    await context.CallActivityAsync("ChargePayment", order);

    await context.CallActivityAsync("SendConfirmation", order);

}
```

Trend 5: Cost Optimization and Operational Efficiency

One of the most cited benefits of serverless is **cost-efficiency**, especially for intermittent or bursty workloads. Azure Functions and Logic Apps charge based on:

- Executions
- Duration (GB-s)
- Triggers used (e.g., Event Hub, HTTP)

Cost-Saving Practices:

- Use consumption plans for unpredictable traffic
- Apply execution timeouts and memory limits

- Move idle APIs from App Service to Functions
- Combine Durable Functions with **externalized state storage**

Monitoring:

- Use **Application Insights** for per-function telemetry
- Configure **alerts** for high execution time or error count
- Use **Azure Advisor** to identify unused or underused serverless resources

---

Trend 6: Infrastructure as Code for Serverless

Deploying serverless components with repeatability is key. Use tools like:

- **Bicep/ARM** **Templates**
- **Terraform** **with** **Azure** **Provider**
- **Pulumi** **for** **code-based** **IaC**
- **GitHub** **Actions** **or** **Azure** **DevOps** **Pipelines**

Example GitHub Workflow for Azure Functions:

```
name: Deploy Function App
on:
  push:
    branches: [main]
jobs:
  deploy:
    runs-on: ubuntu-latest
    steps:
      - uses: actions/checkout@v2
```

```
- uses: Azure/functions-action@v1

  with:

    app-name: 'my-function-app'

    publish-profile: ${{ secrets.AZURE_PUBLISH_PROFILE }}

    package: '.'
```

Trend 7: Serverless Meets Edge and Hybrid

Serverless capabilities are now expanding beyond the cloud. Use:

- **Azure Arc** to run Functions and Logic Apps on-prem or other clouds
- **Azure Stack Edge** to run serverless workloads close to IoT devices
- **Azure Container Apps with VNET** for hybrid networking

Use Case:

- Retail store camera streams → inferencing container on Stack Edge → result sent to Azure via Event Grid → trigger Azure Function → update dashboard

---

Challenges and Considerations

Despite its benefits, serverless architecture has trade-offs:

- **Cold starts**: First invocation latency
- **State management**: Complex for long-running flows
- **Debugging**: Harder across distributed functions
- **Vendor lock-in**: Proprietary runtimes and triggers
- **Observability**: Needs full instrumentation

Mitigation Strategies:

- Use Premium plans or pre-warmed instances
- Externalize state (e.g., Cosmos DB, Storage)
- Use centralized logging with Application Insights
- Use **abstractions** (e.g., Dapr) for portability

Future Outlook

Serverless is evolving toward:

- **Composable microservices** (Functions + Dapr + API Gateway)
- **Low-code/no-code fusion** (Logic Apps + Power Platform)
- **AI/ML-triggered automation** (e.g., Azure OpenAI in Functions)
- **Cross-cloud execution** via open standards (OpenFunction, WASM)
- **Green computing focus** via scale-to-zero and optimized runtimes

---

Conclusion

Serverless computing is maturing rapidly and becoming a primary choice for modern application development. Azure offers a rich serverless ecosystem that supports a variety of workloads—from simple automation scripts to scalable, distributed systems.

As organizations shift toward agility, cost-efficiency, and faster innovation, embracing serverless trends will not only reduce operational complexity but unlock the full potential of event-driven, composable architectures. The key is understanding the right use cases, choosing the correct services, and architecting with observability and governance in mind.

In the next section, we'll explore the cutting edge of computing—quantum and edge solutions—and how Azure is shaping the future with services designed to push the boundaries of what's possible.

Quantum and Edge Computing on Azure

As the boundaries of digital transformation expand, enterprises are beginning to embrace next-generation computing paradigms: **quantum computing** and **edge computing**. Both represent a significant leap beyond conventional cloud capabilities—one in computational power, the other in latency reduction and locality.

Microsoft Azure is uniquely positioned to support both paradigms through its **Azure Quantum platform** and a robust set of **edge computing services**, including Azure Stack Edge, Azure IoT, Azure Arc, and 5G integrations. These offerings unlock opportunities in industries ranging from finance and pharmaceuticals to manufacturing, autonomous vehicles, and space exploration.

In this section, we examine how Azure is enabling organizations to explore and adopt quantum and edge technologies through real-world scenarios, development frameworks, deployment patterns, and integration with existing Azure infrastructure.

The Azure Quantum Ecosystem

Azure Quantum is Microsoft's full-stack, open cloud ecosystem for **quantum computing development, simulation, and experimentation**. It provides access to:

- Quantum hardware from providers like IonQ, Quantinuum, Rigetti, and Microsoft's own future topological qubits

- Quantum simulators for development and testing

- A domain-specific language: **Q#**

- Hybrid workflows that integrate quantum and classical code

Key Components:

- **Azure Quantum Workspace**: Central hub for managing quantum jobs

- **Q# Language and SDK**: Microsoft's quantum programming toolkit

- **Quantum Development Kit (QDK)**: Libraries, simulators, and extensions

- **Jupyter Notebooks + VS Code Extension** for development

- **Classical compute integration** for pre/post-processing using Python, .NET, etc.

Q# Language and Hybrid Code Samples

Q# (pronounced "Q-sharp") is a domain-specific language tailored for expressing quantum algorithms.

Example Q# Program – Basic Quantum Operation:

```
operation HelloQuantum() : Result {

    using (q = Qubit()) {

        H(q);              // Apply Hadamard gate

        let r = M(q);   // Measure qubit

        Reset(q);

        return r;

    }

}
```

Q# programs are often executed alongside classical code using Python or C#, facilitating hybrid quantum-classical algorithms.

Python Integration Example:

```
from qsharp import compile

HelloQuantum = compile("""

    operation HelloQuantum() : Result {

        using (q = Qubit()) {

            H(q);

            let r = M(q);

            Reset(q);

            return r;

        }

    }

""")
```

```
result = HelloQuantum.simulate()

print("Result:", result)
```

Real-World Quantum Use Cases

While universal quantum computing is still maturing, today's quantum simulators and early quantum devices can already be used for:

- **Portfolio optimization** in finance

- **Molecule simulation** in pharmaceuticals

- **Logistics optimization** (e.g., vehicle routing)

- **Pattern recognition** in high-dimensional data

- **Monte Carlo simulations** with accelerated performance

Microsoft's hybrid approach allows companies to explore quantum readiness without waiting for full-scale fault-tolerant hardware.

Azure Quantum Development Workflow

1. **Define workspace** via Azure Portal or CLI

2. **Install QDK and setup dev environment**

3. **Write Q# and host language (Python/.NET) hybrid code**

4. **Simulate locally or on Azure**

5. **Submit job to quantum provider backend**

6. **Retrieve and visualize results**

Azure CLI example:

```
az quantum workspace create \
  --resource-group quantumRG \
```

```
--name myQuantumWS \

--location westus \

--provider microsoft-qc \

--storage-account mystorage
```

Quantum-Inspired Optimization (QIO)

For many organizations, quantum hardware may be years away—but **quantum-inspired optimization algorithms** can run today on classical hardware using Azure.

Use Azure QIO for:

- Supply chain optimization

- Scheduling and resource allocation

- Workforce management

Key Benefit:

- Brings quantum algorithmic benefits **now**, without quantum hardware

Tooling:

- Azure QIO SDK (Python)

- Direct integration with Azure ML and Synapse Analytics

Edge Computing Overview

Edge computing pushes data processing and decision-making closer to the data source—often on-site, at branch locations, or in field environments—rather than routing everything to centralized cloud data centers.

Azure Edge ecosystem includes:

- **Azure Stack Edge**: Ruggedized appliance with AI inferencing, Kubernetes, and FPGA support

- **Azure IoT Edge**: Runtime and modules to push cloud intelligence to edge devices

- **Azure Arc**: Manage edge and on-prem resources as Azure-native entities

- **5G MEC (Multi-access Edge Compute)**: Deploy applications at telco edge sites

- **Azure Sphere**: Secure MCU platform for deeply embedded IoT edge scenarios

---

Edge Architecture Patterns

1. **Preprocessing at the Edge**: Raw IoT data is filtered, aggregated, or enriched locally before being sent to the cloud.

2. **Offline-first Applications**: Edge devices store and sync data intermittently based on connectivity.

3. **AI at the Edge**: ML models are deployed to devices for low-latency decision-making (e.g., anomaly detection, image classification).

4. **Federated Learning**: Edge nodes train local models and send updates, preserving data privacy.

Azure Stack Edge Use Case

Scenario: Factory floor using vision-based AI for product quality control.

Architecture:

- Industrial cameras feed real-time data into **Azure Stack Edge**

- Local AI model (ONNX format) classifies defects

- Acceptable products continue on conveyor

- Defects logged and synced to **Azure Blob Storage**

- **Azure Monitor** tracks edge performance and throughput

Deployment:

- Use Azure ML to train and export model
- Deploy via IoT Hub or Azure Arc
- Inference via Azure Functions on edge device

Azure IoT Edge and DAPR

Deploying microservices and apps to edge devices using **IoT Edge Runtime** or **Dapr** enables a distributed event-driven architecture with built-in observability.

Features:

- Docker-based deployment of custom modules
- Local message routing
- Azure Modules (e.g., Stream Analytics, ML Inference, Twin Synchronization)

Example Manifest:

```json
{
  "modulesContent": {
    "$edgeAgent": {
      "properties.desired": {
        "modules": {
          "mlModule": {
            "settings": {
              "image": "myacr.azurecr.io/ml-inference:latest"
            },
            "type": "docker"
          }
        }
```

```
        }

      }

    }

}
```

Edge + AI Development Workflow

1. Train model in Azure ML

2. Convert to ONNX or TensorRT format

3. Register model in Azure ML or container registry

4. Push to Azure Stack Edge or IoT device

5. Monitor with Azure Monitor and Device Provisioning Service (DPS)

Hybrid Integration and Governance

Azure Arc provides **a control plane for managing edge resources** as part of your Azure environment.

Capabilities:

- Policy enforcement

- RBAC and identity federation

- GitOps-based configuration deployment

- Security compliance tracking

Use Cases:

- Central IT governance for remote retail sites

- Patch management for IoT clusters

- Data residency compliance enforcement

Security and Compliance Considerations

- Use **Hardware Root of Trust** with Azure Sphere and Trusted Platform Modules (TPM)
- Encrypt all device and transmission data (TLS 1.2+)
- Enable **Just-in-Time** access to devices using Azure Defender for IoT
- Monitor edge devices with **Sentinel**, **Azure Monitor**, and **Security Center**

Future Outlook

Quantum:

- Topological qubits promise higher fidelity and scalability
- Standardization of hybrid workflows
- More domain-specific libraries (finance, chemistry, optimization)
- Cross-cloud quantum abstraction APIs

Edge:

- Rise of **autonomous systems** (drones, vehicles, robots)
- Explosion of **edge-native ML models**
- Greater integration with **5G/6G** for ultra-low-latency use cases
- Growth in **decentralized identity** and **zero-trust architectures**

Conclusion

Azure's investments in quantum and edge computing signal a future where computing isn't confined to centralized data centers. Quantum computing redefines what's possible in problem-solving, while edge computing brings intelligence directly to the real world. These technologies—once theoretical—are now tangible tools in the enterprise arsenal.

Architects and developers who prepare today will be the leaders of tomorrow's transformation, where compute is not just fast or scalable—but intelligent, responsive, and everywhere. In the final section of this chapter, we'll explore how to build systems and teams prepared for ongoing, continuous innovation in the cloud.

Preparing for Continuous Innovation

In the rapidly evolving landscape of cloud computing, static architectures are no longer sufficient. Organizations must build systems—and teams—that can **continuously adapt, evolve, and improve**. Continuous innovation is not just about deploying new features quickly; it's about fostering a culture, architecture, and process that enables ongoing change without sacrificing stability, security, or performance.

Azure offers a rich ecosystem to support this mindset: from agile infrastructure and deployment tools to observability, governance, and feedback loops. This section explores how architects can design for continuous innovation using Azure's services, development practices, and organizational models.

The Pillars of Continuous Innovation

Continuous innovation requires alignment across four key domains:

1. **Agile Development Practices**

2. **Composable and Modular Architectures**

3. **Automated Delivery and Observability**

4. **Culture of Experimentation and Feedback**

Each domain must work in tandem to ensure an architecture that supports not just rapid delivery, but sustainable progress.

Agile Development at Scale

Agile practices form the backbone of innovation. Teams must be empowered to experiment, deploy, fail safely, and iterate quickly.

Core Practices:

- Short, iterative sprints (Scrum, Kanban)

- Test-Driven Development (TDD) and Behavior-Driven Development (BDD)

- Shift-left on security and quality

- Feature toggles and canary releases

Azure Tools:

- **Azure DevOps Boards** for backlog tracking

- **GitHub Projects** and Issues for developer-centric planning

- **Azure Test Plans** and **Load Testing** for shift-left validation

Best Practices:

- Keep stories small and independently deployable

- Validate with automated tests before merging to main

- Use pull request policies and required approvals

Building for Change: Composable Architectures

Modular, decoupled systems are easier to update, scale, and evolve. Azure enables composable systems via:

- **Microservices** using Azure Kubernetes Service or Container Apps

- **Serverless functions** for lightweight, atomic business logic

- **API-first design** with Azure API Management

- **Event-driven** communication with Event Grid and Service Bus

- **Domain-driven design** for bounded contexts and clear ownership

Pattern Example:

- Authentication as a shared Azure Function across multiple apps

- Product catalog and inventory as independently deployed microservices

- Cross-service communication via **Event Grid topics**

Benefits:

- Parallel development across teams

- Minimized blast radius during deployments

- Easier to test, monitor, and evolve in isolation

Continuous Integration and Continuous Delivery (CI/CD)

Automation is essential to scale innovation. CI/CD pipelines reduce friction in delivery, enforce quality, and promote consistency.

CI/CD Toolchain on Azure:

- **GitHub Actions** or **Azure DevOps Pipelines**

- **Azure Container Registry (ACR)** for container builds

- **Azure Key Vault** for secrets management

- **Bicep, ARM, or Terraform** for infrastructure provisioning

- **Feature management** with Azure App Configuration

Sample GitHub Action for Azure App Service:

```
name: Deploy to App Service

on:

  push:

    branches:

      - main

jobs:

  build-and-deploy:
```

```
runs-on: ubuntu-latest

steps:

- uses: actions/checkout@v2

- uses: azure/webapps-deploy@v2

  with:

    app-name: 'myapp'

    publish-profile: ${{ secrets.AZURE_WEBAPP_PUBLISH_PROFILE }}

    package: '.'
```

Best Practices:

- Promote infrastructure and application in parallel
- Implement blue-green or canary deployments
- Automate rollbacks on failure signals
- Integrate testing into every stage of the pipeline

Observability and Feedback Loops

You can't improve what you can't observe. Observability is the foundation of operational excellence and ongoing innovation.

Azure Observability Stack:

- **Azure Monitor** for metrics and alerts
- **Application Insights** for request tracing, failures, and usage
- **Log Analytics** for centralized log querying
- **Azure Workbooks** for dashboards
- **Azure Sentinel** for security analytics

Operational Metrics to Monitor:

- Latency and throughput
- Error rates (5xx responses, failed function executions)
- Resource utilization (CPU, memory, IOPS)
- Cost and budget alerts
- Feature usage via custom telemetry

Example KQL Query (Log Analytics):

```
requests
| where timestamp > ago(24h)
| summarize count() by cloud_RoleName, resultCode
```

Feedback Channels:

- Use **UserVoice**, **Azure DevOps**, or **GitHub Discussions** for product feedback
- Collect telemetry on feature usage
- Interview stakeholders regularly and include feedback in backlog

---

Governance Without Friction

To innovate safely, teams need **guardrails**—not gates. Azure provides governance tools that support innovation without central bottlenecks.

Azure Governance Tools:

- **Azure Policy** for enforcing standards (e.g., tag requirements, location restrictions)
- **Azure Blueprints** for environment consistency
- **Management Groups** for organizational hierarchy
- **Cost Management** for financial accountability

- **Azure Lighthouse** for external partners and MSPs

Use Case: Automatically enforce policy that disallows creation of public-facing storage accounts:

```
{

  "if": {

    "field":
"Microsoft.Storage/storageAccounts/networkAcls.defaultAction",

    "equals": "Allow"

  },

  "then": {

    "effect": "deny"

  }

}
```

Best Practices:

- Define guardrails early and communicate clearly
- Empower teams with **self-service environments**
- Use tags and naming conventions to support reporting
- Apply least-privilege RBAC and review frequently

Cultivating an Innovation Culture

People and process are just as important as technology. A culture of innovation requires:

- Psychological safety to experiment and fail
- Blameless postmortems and retrospectives

- Encouragement of continuous learning
- Cross-functional teams that own products end-to-end
- Engineering leaders that reward risk-taking and collaboration

Organizational Models:

- **Spotify model** (Squads, Tribes, Chapters)
- **Platform teams** that build reusable services and tools
- **Product-aligned teams** that ship vertical slices of functionality

Team Rituals:

- Weekly demos of work in progress
- Retrospectives with real-time feedback loops
- Monthly innovation sprints or hackathons
- Technical debt reviews and architectural runway planning

Measuring Innovation Effectiveness

To ensure innovation translates into value, define **Key Performance Indicators (KPIs)** such as:

- Deployment frequency
- Lead time for changes
- Change failure rate
- Mean time to restore (MTTR)
- Feature adoption rates
- Customer satisfaction (CSAT/NPS)
- Developer experience (DevEx surveys)

Visualize trends using **Power BI**, **Grafana**, or Azure Dashboards.

Looking Ahead

Azure continues to release tools that foster innovation:

- **Azure Developer CLI (azd)**: Scaffolds full-stack apps with infra + CI/CD

- **Azure Chaos Studio**: Introduces controlled failure to test resilience

- **AI-assisted development**: GitHub Copilot and Azure OpenAI APIs

- **Dapr + Container Apps**: Building block model for modern microservices

- **Azure Workload Identity**: Seamless identity flow in Kubernetes and beyond

---

Conclusion

Preparing for continuous innovation means building systems that are not only resilient and scalable—but also **adaptable by design**. By leveraging Azure's extensive tooling, aligning with agile principles, and fostering a strong engineering culture, organizations can transform innovation from a buzzword into a repeatable, measurable practice.

This future-forward mindset ensures that businesses are not just reacting to change—but leading it. Whether launching new features, experimenting with disruptive tech, or responding to customer insights, the ability to innovate continuously is now the defining competitive advantage in the cloud era.

Chapter 11: Appendices

Glossary of Terms

A strong understanding of key terminology is essential when navigating the landscape of Azure and cloud architecture. This glossary provides definitions and context for common terms used throughout this book. Whether you're a seasoned architect or a newcomer to cloud computing, having a reference for acronyms, services, patterns, and protocols will strengthen your comprehension and help you communicate effectively across teams.

API   (Application   Programming   Interface)
A set of protocols and tools that allow different software applications to communicate. In cloud architecture, APIs are used to interact with services like Azure REST APIs or to expose microservices through Azure API Management.

ARM   (Azure   Resource   Manager)
The deployment and management service for Azure. It provides a consistent management layer to create, update, and delete resources using templates (ARM templates), CLI, PowerShell, or SDKs.

Availability   Zone
Physically separate zones within an Azure region, each with its own power, cooling, and networking. Deploying across zones increases availability and fault tolerance.

Azure   Arc
A service that extends Azure management and governance to on-premises, multi-cloud, and edge environments. Arc allows you to manage servers, Kubernetes clusters, and data services from the Azure portal.

Azure   DevOps
A suite of development tools for planning, developing, testing, and delivering applications. It includes Boards, Repos, Pipelines, Test Plans, and Artifacts.

Azure   Front   Door
A global application delivery network service that provides fast, secure, and scalable routing

of HTTP(S) requests. It supports features like global load balancing, SSL offloading, WAF, and URL-based routing.

Azure   **Kubernetes**   **Service**   **(AKS)**
A managed Kubernetes service that simplifies deployment, management, and operations of Kubernetes clusters in Azure. It supports features like auto-scaling, node pools, and integrated CI/CD pipelines.

Azure   **Logic**   **Apps**
A serverless platform for automating workflows and integrating systems through a visual designer. Supports hundreds of connectors including SQL, Salesforce, SAP, and custom APIs.

Azure   **Monitor**
A comprehensive monitoring solution that collects telemetry from applications and infrastructure. It includes metrics, logs, traces, and alerts, and integrates with Application Insights and Log Analytics.

Azure   **Resource**   **Group**
A container that holds related Azure resources. It provides a way to manage and organize resources collectively based on lifecycle, environment, or function.

Azure   **SQL**   **Database**
A fully managed relational database-as-a-service built on Microsoft SQL Server. Offers features like automatic tuning, geo-replication, and threat detection.

Azure   **Storage**   **Account**
A core storage service in Azure supporting blobs, files, queues, and tables. It is used for storing structured and unstructured data, including media, backups, logs, and telemetry.

Bicep
A domain-specific language (DSL) for declarative deployment of Azure resources. It offers a simplified syntax over ARM templates and supports modularization and code reuse.

CDN   (Content   Delivery   Network)
A network of distributed servers that deliver content to users based on geographic proximity. Azure CDN helps reduce latency and increase performance for static content delivery.

CI/CD   (Continuous   Integration   /   Continuous   Delivery)
A DevOps practice that automates the building, testing, and deployment of applications. Azure DevOps and GitHub Actions support CI/CD pipelines for rapid delivery of software changes.

Cloud   Adoption   Framework   (CAF)
Microsoft's proven guidance to help organizations adopt Azure. It includes strategy, planning, readiness, governance, and management best practices.

Cloud-native
An approach to building and running applications that fully leverage the advantages of the cloud model, such as elasticity, scalability, and resilience. Includes technologies like containers, serverless, and microservices.

Cognitive   Services
A suite of AI APIs and SDKs in Azure for tasks like vision, language understanding, speech processing, and decision-making.

Container   Registry   (ACR)
A managed Docker container registry in Azure that stores and manages private container images and artifacts used for container-based deployments.

Durable   Functions
An extension of Azure Functions that enables stateful workflows. Supports patterns like function chaining, fan-out/fan-in, and human interaction.

Event   Grid
A fully managed event routing service that enables event-driven architectures. Supports system and custom topics, subscribers, and filtering.

ExpressRoute
A private connection between your on-premises network and Azure datacenters. Provides higher reliability, faster speeds, and lower latencies than public internet connections.

Function   App
The hosting environment for Azure Functions. Supports different plans like Consumption, Premium, and Dedicated (App Service) for flexible scaling and cost management.

Hybrid   Cloud
A computing environment that combines public cloud, private cloud, and on-premises infrastructure, allowing data and applications to be shared across them.

IAM   (Identity   and   Access   Management)
Azure's system for defining who can access what resources, and under what conditions. Includes Role-Based Access Control (RBAC), Azure AD, Conditional Access, and Privileged Identity Management (PIM).

Infrastructure   as   Code   (IaC)
The practice of managing infrastructure through code rather than manual processes. Azure supports IaC via Bicep, ARM templates, Terraform, and Pulumi.

KEDA   (Kubernetes-based   Event-Driven   Autoscaler)
A component that enables Kubernetes workloads to scale based on events from Azure services like Event Hub, Service Bus, or custom metrics.

Key   Vault
A service to securely store and manage application secrets, encryption keys, and certificates. Integrates with managed identities and policies for fine-grained access control.

Managed   Identity
A feature of Azure Active Directory that allows Azure services to authenticate to other Azure services without storing credentials in code.

Microservices
An architectural style that structures an application as a collection of loosely coupled services, each responsible for a specific functionality and independently deployable.

NSG (Network Security Group)
A security rule container that controls inbound and outbound traffic to network interfaces, VMs, and subnets. Acts as a firewall at the virtual network level.

PaaS (Platform as a Service)
A cloud computing model that delivers application development platforms and tools over the internet. Azure App Service and Azure SQL Database are examples.

RBAC (Role-Based Access Control)
An authorization system that manages user permissions based on assigned roles. Azure RBAC ensures least-privilege access to resources.

Resource Lock
A mechanism to prevent accidental deletion or modification of Azure resources. Supports two modes: ReadOnly and CanNotDelete.

Serverless
A cloud-native model where application code runs in response to events and automatically scales. Azure Functions and Logic Apps are primary examples.

Service Bus
An enterprise messaging service that facilitates communication between decoupled applications and services. Supports queues, topics, and dead-lettering.

Terraform
An open-source IaC tool used to define and provision infrastructure using declarative configuration files. Supports Azure through the AzureRM provider.

Virtual   Network   (VNet)
The fundamental building block of Azure networking, allowing secure communication between Azure resources, the internet, and on-premises networks.

VPN   Gateway
Connects on-premises networks to Azure through site-to-site VPNs using IPsec/IKE protocol.

Workbooks
Interactive reports built on top of Azure Monitor logs, allowing teams to create dashboards for performance, availability, and usage insights.

This glossary is designed to be a living reference that readers can revisit throughout their cloud journey. It is particularly useful when navigating documentation, collaborating across technical domains, or preparing for Azure certifications. Understanding this vocabulary builds the foundation for designing, deploying, and managing resilient, scalable cloud architectures.

Resources for Further Learning

The field of cloud architecture is dynamic, with constant evolution in services, tools, and best practices. Continuous learning is essential to remain effective as an Azure architect. Microsoft and the broader tech community offer an extensive set of resources that support professional development at every stage—whether you're just starting with Azure or looking to deepen your expertise in specialized domains such as DevOps, security, data, or AI.

This section compiles a curated set of official documentation, certifications, online courses, books, communities, blogs, YouTube channels, and podcasts to help you maintain and grow your Azure knowledge. These resources are organized by format and topic for easy reference and accessibility.

Official Microsoft Learning Platforms

Microsoft Learn

Microsoft Learn is Microsoft's official learning platform offering interactive, hands-on learning paths and modules.

Key Features:

- Free   and   self-paced

- Integrated with sandbox environments for labs

- Tracks your learning progress and skill achievements

- Includes role-based and product-based training

Recommended Learning Paths:

- Azure Fundamentals

- Azure Architect Design

- Azure Administrator

- DevOps Engineer Expert

- Designing and Implementing a Hybrid Networking Strategy

Microsoft Documentation

Microsoft Docs (now part of Microsoft Learn) provides comprehensive technical documentation for all Azure services, including tutorials, API references, architecture guidance, and FAQs.

Tips:

- Bookmark the landing pages for frequently used services (e.g., Azure Functions, Cosmos DB)

- Check the "Quickstart" and "How-to" guides for implementation patterns

- Subscribe to release notes and RSS feeds for updates

Certifications and Exams

Microsoft's role-based certifications validate your knowledge and skills across various job roles.

Popular Azure Certifications:

- **AZ-900**: Microsoft Certified: Azure Fundamentals

- **AZ-104**: Azure Administrator Associate

- **AZ-305**: Azure Solutions Architect Expert
- **AZ-400**: DevOps Engineer Expert
- **AI-102**: Azure AI Engineer Associate
- **SC-300**: Identity and Access Administrator
- **DP-203**: Data Engineering on Azure

Certification Resources:

- Microsoft Learn certification prep paths
- MeasureUp and Whizlabs practice exams
- Pluralsight, Udemy, and LinkedIn Learning courses
- Exam-specific study guides and whitepapers

Online Courses and Video Series

Free Platforms

- **YouTube** – Microsoft Azure channel, John Savill's Technical Training, Cloud Academy, and FreeCodeCamp
- **Channel 9 / Microsoft Learn TV** – Deep dives, Ignite sessions, and event recordings

Paid Platforms

- **Pluralsight** – High-quality courses by Microsoft MVPs, structured paths, and assessments
- **A Cloud Guru** – Strong focus on cloud certifications, labs, and real-world scenarios
- **LinkedIn Learning** – Courses tied to career development and soft skills
- **Udemy** – Affordable, up-to-date courses for specific exams and services

---

Books and Whitepapers

Books offer deep, structured learning and often include design patterns, sample projects, and certification prep.

Recommended Titles:

- *Exam Ref AZ-305 Designing Microsoft Azure Infrastructure Solutions* by Ashish Agrawal

- *Azure Architecture Explained* by Peter De Tender

- *Cloud Architecture Patterns* by Bill Wilder

- *The Phoenix Project* & *The DevOps Handbook* by Gene Kim (DevOps)

- *Microsoft Azure Essentials* series (free eBooks)

Where to Find:

- Microsoft Press

- Amazon Kindle Store

- O'Reilly Media (also available via Safari subscription)

- Packt Publishing

Architecture and Design Resources

Azure Architecture Center

Azure Architecture Center is the central hub for reference architectures, design patterns, best practices, and cloud adoption guidance.

Key Sections:

- Reference architectures (e.g., Microservices, AKS, Web App)

- Well-Architected Framework

- Cloud Adoption Framework (CAF)

- Industry-specific solutions (Healthcare, Retail, Finance)

- Resiliency, security, and governance blueprints

Azure Well-Architected Review Tool

Evaluate your workloads against Azure's five pillars:

- Reliability

- Security

- Cost   Optimization

- Operational   Excellence

- Performance   Efficiency

Find the tool here: https://aka.ms/azreview

GitHub and Code Samples

GitHub repositories are essential for practical learning and reference implementations.

Key Repositories:

- Azure   Samples

- Azure   Quickstart   Templates

- Azure   Bicep   Examples

- [Terraform Azure Modules](https://github.com/Azure/terraform-azurerm-* modules)

Clone these to practice deployments, review syntax, and contribute to open source projects.

Blogs and Community Content

Following expert blogs keeps you up to date with trends, tricks, and upcoming changes.

Microsoft Blogs:

- Azure   Blog

- Tech   Community

- Developer   Blogs

MVP and Expert Blogs:

- Thomas   Maurer   (Azure   Arc,   Hybrid)

- Scott   Hanselman   (Developer   productivity)

- Troy   Hunt   (Security   &   Identity)

- Christos   Matskas   (Identity/Access   &   .NET)

- Sam   Cogan   (Infrastructure   &   DevOps)

Podcasts

Learn on the go by subscribing to these popular Azure and cloud podcasts:

- **Azure Friday** – Hosted by Scott Hanselman, short episodes on services and teams behind   Azure

- **The Azure Podcast** – Weekly episodes from Azure engineering and field teams

- **CloudSkills.fm** – Focuses on cloud career growth and DevOps

- **Microsoft Cloud Show** – Covers Azure, Microsoft 365, and development topics

- **Architecting the Cloud** – Strategic conversations around enterprise cloud design

Events and Certifications Programs

- **Microsoft Ignite** – Annual flagship conference with keynotes, workshops, and product announcements

- **Microsoft Build** – Developer-focused event on apps, tools, and Azure services

- **Microsoft Reactor** – Local and virtual meetups, workshops, and community-led sessions

- **Cloud Skills Challenge** – Time-boxed Learn challenges with free exam vouchers

Subscribe to Microsoft Events Calendar: https://events.microsoft.com/

Community and Networking

Learning doesn't have to be solitary. The Azure community is vibrant, global, and welcoming.

- Join the **Microsoft Tech Community**
- Participate in **Reddit r/AZURE, Stack Overflow**, and **LinkedIn groups**
- Attend **Azure Meetups** (check via meetup.com)
- Contribute to **GitHub Discussions** and **Open Source Projects**

Staying Current

The Azure platform evolves rapidly. To keep up:

- Follow Azure and service-specific **Twitter/X accounts**
- Enable **RSS notifications** on Azure Updates
- Use **Azure Updates page** for change tracking: https://azure.microsoft.com/en-us/updates/
- Subscribe to **Azure newsletter** or Microsoft Cloud Blog Digest

---

Conclusion

This compilation of learning resources is designed to be your launchpad for mastering Azure and staying up to date with the latest innovations. Whether you prefer structured learning paths, hands-on coding, or community-driven discussions, there are countless ways to grow. Cloud architecture is a journey, not a destination—and your commitment to continuous learning is the most powerful tool you have.

Bookmark this section, share it with your team, and revisit it frequently as both your skills and Azure itself continue to evolve.

Sample Projects and Code Snippets

One of the most effective ways to solidify your understanding of Azure architecture is by building real-world projects. This section presents a range of sample projects—each accompanied by practical code snippets—that reflect common scenarios architects and developers encounter in modern cloud environments. The goal is not only to demonstrate technical implementation but also to highlight architectural decisions, patterns, and trade-offs.

These projects span web apps, APIs, event-driven systems, microservices, hybrid workloads, and serverless solutions. You can use them as references, templates, or starting points for your own work, whether for learning, prototyping, or production deployment.

Project 1: Scalable Web App with CI/CD Pipeline

Objective: Build a scalable web application hosted on Azure App Service, backed by Azure SQL Database, and deployed via GitHub Actions.

Components:

- Azure App Service
- Azure SQL Database
- Azure Key Vault
- Azure Monitor
- GitHub Actions for CI/CD

Architecture:

1. Frontend (React) served via App Service
2. Backend API (.NET or Node.js) exposes endpoints
3. Secrets managed in Key Vault
4. SQL database stores relational data
5. Application Insights tracks logs and performance

Deployment Workflow:

```
name: Build and Deploy Web App
```

```yaml
on:
  push:
    branches:
      - main

jobs:
  deploy:
    runs-on: ubuntu-latest
    steps:
      - name: Checkout code
        uses: actions/checkout@v2

      - name: Login to Azure
        uses: azure/login@v1
        with:
          creds: ${{ secrets.AZURE_CREDENTIALS }}

      - name: Deploy to Azure Web App
        uses: azure/webapps-deploy@v2
        with:
          app-name: 'my-web-app'
          publish-profile: ${{ secrets.AZURE_WEBAPP_PUBLISH_PROFILE }}
          package: '.'
```

Project 2: Event-Driven Order Processing System

Objective: Process e-commerce orders asynchronously using Azure Functions and Service Bus.

Components:

- Azure Function App
- Azure Service Bus (Queue + Topic)
- Azure Cosmos DB (for order state)
- Application Insights
- Azure Storage (for order confirmations)

Architecture:

1. Order submission triggers Service Bus message
2. Azure Function processes message and stores order
3. Topic notifies fulfillment and email subsystems
4. Confirmation blob uploaded to Azure Storage

Function Snippet:

```
[FunctionName("ProcessOrder")]

public static async Task Run(

  [ServiceBusTrigger("orders", Connection = "SBConnection")] string message,

  ILogger log)

{

    var order = JsonConvert.DeserializeObject<Order>(message);

    // Store in Cosmos DB, process logic

    log.LogInformation($"Order {order.Id} processed.");
```

```
}
```

Project 3: Hybrid Cloud File Sync with Azure File Share

Objective: Extend an on-premises file server using Azure File Sync for cloud backup and disaster recovery.

Components:

- On-prem Windows Server
- Azure File Storage
- Azure File Sync Agent
- Azure Recovery Services Vault

Workflow:

1. Install File Sync agent and register server
2. Create Azure File Share and sync group
3. Configure tiering policy (cloud-first, frequently accessed stays local)
4. Backup file share to Recovery Vault

PowerShell Snippet:

```
Register-AzStorageSyncServer -ResourceGroupName "myRG" `

    -StorageSyncServiceName "mySyncService" `

    -ServerName "OnPremFS"


New-AzStorageSyncGroup -ResourceGroupName "myRG" `

    -StorageSyncServiceName "mySyncService" `

    -SyncGroupName "myFileGroup"
```

Project 4: Serverless API Gateway with Rate Limiting

Objective: Expose Azure Functions through API Management with OAuth2 authentication and request throttling.

Components:

- Azure   API   Management
- Azure   Functions   (HTTP   trigger)
- Azure   App   Insights
- Azure   AD   B2C   for   identity

API Policy Snippet:

```
<inbound>

    <base />

    <rate-limit-by-key calls="10" renewal-period="60" counter-key="@(context.Request.IpAddress)" />

    <validate-jwt header-name="Authorization" failed-validation-httpcode="401">

        <openid-config url="https://<your-tenant>.b2clogin.com/.../.well-known/openid-configuration" />

        <required-claims>

            <claim name="aud">

                <value>api://my-api-id</value>

            </claim>

        </required-claims>

    </validate-jwt>

</inbound>
```

Benefits:

- Low-cost   and   scalable
- Centralized   auth   and   monitoring
- Secure   backend   services

Project 5: Microservices with Azure Kubernetes Service (AKS)

Objective: Deploy a polyglot microservice architecture on AKS using internal ingress, Dapr for service-to-service calls, and Azure Monitor.

Components:

- AKS   with   Azure   CNI
- NGINX   Ingress   Controller
- Azure   Container   Registry   (ACR)
- Dapr   Sidecars
- Application   Gateway   (optional)

Deployment Steps:

1. Deploy   AKS   via   Terraform   or   Bicep
2. Push   images   to   ACR
3. Use   Helm   to   deploy   microservices
4. Enable   Dapr   annotations   for   sidecar   injection

Helm Deployment Example:

```
helm install inventory-service ./charts/inventory \
  --set image.repository=myregistry.azurecr.io/inventory \
  --set image.tag=latest
```

Dapr Annotation:

```
annotations:

  dapr.io/enabled: "true"

  dapr.io/app-id: "inventory-service"

  dapr.io/app-port: "5000"
```

Project 6: Identity-Enabled SPA with Azure AD

Objective: Build a secure single-page application (SPA) with Azure AD B2C authentication and protected backend APIs.

Stack:

- React   SPA   frontend

- ASP.NET   Core   Web   API

- Azure   AD   B2C

- MSAL.js   for   frontend   auth

MSAL Frontend Snippet:

```
const msalInstance = new PublicClientApplication({

  auth: {

    clientId: "your-client-id",

    authority:
"https://<tenant>.b2clogin.com/<tenant>.onmicrosoft.com/B2C_1_signup
signin",

    redirectUri: "http://localhost:3000"

  }

});
```

```
const loginRequest = {

  scopes: ["openid", "profile", "api://your-api-client-id/access"]

};
```

```
msalInstance.loginRedirect(loginRequest);
```

Backend:

- Protect with `[Authorize]` and validate token against Azure AD metadata

---

Project 7: Data Pipeline with Azure Synapse and Data Factory

Objective: Ingest, transform, and analyze data from a SaaS platform using Azure Data Factory and Synapse Analytics.

Pipeline Overview:

1. Ingest CSV from SFTP via Self-hosted Integration Runtime

2. Transform with Synapse SQL Pool or Spark

3. Load into Azure Data Lake and Power BI

ADF Copy Activity JSON Snippet:

```
{

  "name": "CopyFromSFTPToLake",

  "type": "Copy",

  "inputs": [{"referenceName": "SFTPInput", "type": "DatasetReference"}],

  "outputs": [{"referenceName": "LakeOutput", "type": "DatasetReference"}],
```

```
"typeProperties": {

  "source": { "type": "DelimitedTextSource" },

  "sink": { "type": "AzureBlobSink" }

}

}
```

Best Practices Across All Projects

- Use **tags** to organize resources
- Secure access via **managed** **identity**
- Enable **cost** **alerts** and **budgets**
- Integrate **Azure** **Monitor** **and** **Log** **Analytics** for observability
- Deploy infrastructure with **Bicep** or **Terraform**
- Use **Key** **Vault** for all secrets and connection strings

Conclusion

These sample projects represent just a few of the many real-world implementations you can build using Azure. Each combines Azure services into cohesive solutions, demonstrating how to solve practical challenges while adhering to architectural best practices.

As you work through or extend these examples, be sure to apply key principles such as automation, observability, cost-awareness, and security by design. These will help you not only prototype effectively but also build production-grade systems that are resilient, maintainable, and scalable.

API Reference Guide

APIs are the foundational layer that enable communication and integration across Azure services and between cloud-based and on-premises systems. Whether you're building a microservice, managing resources, triggering automation, or enabling external access to your data and functionality, a solid understanding of Azure APIs and how to consume them is essential.

This API Reference Guide outlines the most commonly used Azure APIs, patterns for authentication and authorization, tools for testing and documenting APIs, and real-world code examples to help you quickly get up and running with secure, scalable, and well-structured APIs.

Types of APIs in Azure

Azure exposes a wide variety of APIs across multiple layers:

- **Management APIs**: Used to provision, manage, and monitor Azure resources (e.g., Azure Resource Manager REST APIs)

- **Service APIs**: Used to interact with specific services like Azure Storage, Cosmos DB, Event Grid, etc.

- **Custom APIs**: APIs you build and expose through Azure API Management or App Services

- **SDKs and Client Libraries**: Wrappers around APIs available for .NET, JavaScript, Python, Java, Go, and more

Authentication and Authorization

Azure supports several methods for securing and authenticating API access.

Azure Active Directory (Azure AD)

Use OAuth 2.0 tokens issued by Azure AD to authenticate applications and users.

Flow Overview:

1. Register application in Azure AD

2. Assign API permissions

3. Acquire token using client credentials or authorization code flow

4. Pass token in Authorization header

Token Request (Client Credentials):

```
POST https://login.microsoftonline.com/{tenant}/oauth2/v2.0/token

Content-Type: application/x-www-form-urlencoded


client_id={client-id}

&scope=https://management.azure.com/.default

&client_secret={client-secret}

&grant_type=client_credentials
```

Use Token in Request:

```
GET
https://management.azure.com/subscriptions/{subscriptionId}/resource
groups?api-version=2021-04-01

Authorization: Bearer {access_token}
```

Shared Access Signature (SAS)

Used for services like Azure Blob Storage and Queue. Grants limited-time, scoped access.

SAS Example for Blob Access:

```
az storage blob generate-sas \

  --account-name mystorage \

  --container-name mycontainer \

  --name myfile.txt \

  --permissions r \

  --expiry 2025-01-01T00:00Z \

  --output tsv
```

Azure Management REST API

Base URL: `https://management.azure.com/`

All requests must include:

- `Authorization:` `Bearer` `{token}`
- `api-version` as a query string

Sample: List Resource Groups:

```
GET /subscriptions/{subscriptionId}/resourcegroups?api-version=2021-04-01
```

Response:

```json
{
  "value": [
    {
      "id": "/subscriptions/xxx/resourceGroups/myGroup",
      "name": "myGroup",
      "location": "eastus",
      "properties": {
        "provisioningState": "Succeeded"
      }
    }
  ]
}
```

Use tools like **Postman**, **curl**, or **Insomnia** for manual testing.

Azure SDKs and Clients

Azure SDKs make it easier to call APIs programmatically.

Install SDK (Python Example):

```
pip install azure-mgmt-resource azure-identity
```

Sample Code to List Resource Groups:

```
from azure.identity import DefaultAzureCredential

from azure.mgmt.resource import ResourceManagementClient


subscription_id = 'your-subscription-id'

credential = DefaultAzureCredential()


client = ResourceManagementClient(credential, subscription_id)


for rg in client.resource_groups.list():

    print(rg.name)
```

SDKs are available for:

- **Management libraries**: ARM, subscriptions, policy
- **Service libraries**: Blob Storage, Cosmos DB, Key Vault
- **Event-driven**: Event Hubs, Service Bus, Event Grid
- **AI & ML**: Cognitive Services, Azure ML, OpenAI

Azure API Management

API Management (APIM) is Azure's full-featured gateway for managing, securing, and scaling APIs.

Key Features:

- Rate limiting and throttling
- OAuth2/JWT validation
- Request/response transformations
- Caching and versioning
- Developer portal with documentation and test console

API Creation Example via Bicep:

```
resource apim 'Microsoft.ApiManagement/service@2022-08-01' = {

  name: 'my-apim'

  location: 'eastus'

  sku: {

    name: 'Developer'

    capacity: 1

  }

  properties: {

    publisherEmail: 'admin@contoso.com'

    publisherName: 'Contoso API Team'

  }

}
```

Common Policy Snippet (CORS):

```
<inbound>

  <base />
```

```
<cors>

  <allowed-origins>

    <origin>*</origin>

  </allowed-origins>

  <allowed-methods>

    <method>GET</method>

    <method>POST</method>

  </allowed-methods>

  </cors>

</inbound>
```

Swagger/OpenAPI Integration

OpenAPI (formerly Swagger) is a widely adopted specification for defining RESTful APIs. Azure supports importing OpenAPI definitions into:

- API   Management

- Azure   Functions   Proxies

- Logic   Apps   Custom   Connectors

Example OpenAPI Snippet:

```
openapi: 3.0.0

info:

  title: Orders API

  version: 1.0.0

paths:

  /orders:
```

```
get:

  summary: Get all orders

  responses:

    '200':

      description: OK
```

Use **Swagger UI**, **Redoc**, or **Stoplight** to generate interactive docs.

Calling Azure APIs from Applications

JavaScript with MSAL.js

```javascript
const msalInstance = new PublicClientApplication(msalConfig);


const tokenRequest = {

  scopes: ["https://management.azure.com/.default"]

};


msalInstance.acquireTokenSilent(tokenRequest).then(response => {

  fetch("https://management.azure.com/subscriptions?api-
version=2021-04-01", {

    headers: {

      Authorization: `Bearer ${response.accessToken}`

    }

  });

});
```

.NET with Azure.Identity

```
var credential = new DefaultAzureCredential();

var client = new ArmClient(credential);

var subscription = client.GetSubscriptions().First();
```

Monitoring API Usage

Monitor API usage with:

- **Azure Monitor** for custom APIs
- **API Management analytics dashboard**
- **Application Insights** for request traces and dependencies
- **Log Analytics** to run KQL queries on HTTP logs

Example KQL:

```
requests

| where url contains "/orders"

| summarize count(), avg(duration) by resultCode
```

API Governance and Security

To ensure API quality and security:

- Use **naming conventions** and versioning (/v1, /v2)
- Validate inputs with JSON Schema or OpenAPI
- Enforce authentication with OAuth2 or certificates
- Apply **rate limiting** and **quotas**

- Log all requests for auditability

- Mask sensitive data in logs

Tools:

- Azure Policy for endpoint control

- Azure Key Vault for secure key storage

- Microsoft Defender for APIs (preview) for threat protection

---

Conclusion

This reference guide offers a comprehensive overview of working with APIs in Azure—from calling management APIs and using SDKs to exposing secure and scalable endpoints via API Management. Understanding these patterns empowers developers and architects to build connected systems that adhere to best practices for observability, maintainability, and security.

APIs are the glue that binds modern cloud applications. Whether you're integrating systems, enabling partners, or building user-facing functionality, mastering Azure APIs is an essential skill for any architect or developer operating in today's digital-first world.

Frequently Asked Questions

As you explore the architecture, services, and capabilities of Microsoft Azure, it's natural to encounter recurring questions—whether technical, strategic, or operational. This section compiles the most frequently asked questions (FAQs) about Azure architecture from the perspective of architects, developers, and IT decision-makers. The answers aim to clarify core concepts, guide best practices, and help you navigate common scenarios with confidence.

Each answer is crafted with practical detail, relevant examples, and references to Azure services or design patterns. This section serves as a go-to resource for clearing doubts quickly, validating assumptions, and building architectural certainty.

What is the difference between IaaS, PaaS, and SaaS on Azure?

- **Infrastructure as a Service (IaaS)**: Provides virtualized computing resources like VMs, storage, and networking. You manage OS, runtime, and apps. (e.g., Azure Virtual Machines)

- **Platform as a Service (PaaS)**: Azure manages infrastructure and OS; you focus on apps. Faster to deploy and scale. (e.g., Azure App Service, Azure Functions)

- **Software as a Service (SaaS)**: Fully managed applications delivered over the internet. (e.g., Microsoft 365, Dynamics 365)

Comparison Table:

Responsibility	IaaS	PaaS	SaaS
Application	✓	✓	✗
Runtime & Middleware	✓	✓	✗
OS & VM	✓	✗	✗
Infrastructure	✓	✓	✓

How do I choose between Azure Functions and Azure App Service?

- Use **Azure Functions** when:
  - You need event-driven, short-lived logic
  - You want pay-per-execution billing
  - You want to scale down to zero when idle
- Use **Azure App Service** when:
  - You need a long-running API or web app
  - You need custom domains, TLS, and integrated CI/CD
  - You need persistent state and background jobs

Example   **Use**   **Case**:
Use Functions to process image uploads, but App Service to host the dashboard UI and REST APIs.

How do I secure secrets and configuration in Azure?

Use **Azure Key Vault** to store:

- Secrets (connection strings, passwords)

- Certificates (SSL/TLS)

- Keys (encryption keys)

Best Practices:

- Use **Managed Identity** to authenticate apps to Key Vault

- Do not store secrets in code or app settings

- Use RBAC or Key Vault access policies to control access

```
az keyvault secret set --vault-name "myVault" --name "DbPassword" --value "p@ssw0rd123"
```

What is the best way to scale an application on Azure?

- **Horizontal Scaling**: Add more instances (App Service, AKS nodes)

- **Vertical Scaling**: Increase VM size or App Plan tier

- **Auto-scaling**: Use rules based on CPU, memory, HTTP requests

- **Geo-scaling**: Use Traffic Manager or Front Door for global distribution

For App Service:

```
az monitor autoscale create \
  --resource-group myRG \
```

```
--resource myAppServicePlan \

--min-count 1 --max-count 5 \

--count 1
```

What's the difference between Azure Front Door and Traffic Manager?

- **Front Door**: Layer 7 HTTP/HTTPS global load balancer. Includes SSL offload, path-based   routing,   and   WAF.

- **Traffic Manager**: DNS-based load balancing, works at layer 4 (IP level). Use for routing across regions based on performance, geography, or failover.

Tip: Use Front Door when routing web traffic; use Traffic Manager for hybrid or cross-cloud workloads.

How can I monitor the health of my Azure application?

Use **Azure Monitor** and **Application Insights**.

Key Metrics:

- Request   rates

- Response   times

- Failure   counts

- Custom   events   and   traces

Tools:

- Alerts   and   autoscale   rules

- Dashboards   via   Azure   Workbooks

- Log   Analytics   for   advanced   queries

Example KQL Query:

```
requests

| where success == false

| summarize count() by operation_Name, resultCode
```

How do I implement high availability in Azure?

- **Use multiple Availability Zones** within a region
- **Deploy across regions** with Traffic Manager or Front Door
- **Use availability sets** for legacy VMs
- **Use geo-replication** for storage and databases
- **Design for statelessness**, use distributed caching (Azure Cache for Redis)

Service-Specific Tips:

- Cosmos DB: Turn on multi-region write
- App Service: Enable zone redundancy in Premium plans
- SQL Database: Use active geo-replication

What's the difference between Azure Cosmos DB and SQL Database?

Feature	Azure SQL Database	Azure Cosmos DB
Data Model	Relational (SQL)	Multi-model (NoSQL, JSON)
Consistency Levels	Strong	5 models (strong to eventual)
Global Distribution	Geo-replication optional	Native multi-region

Use Case	Traditional apps	Real-time IoT, mobile, AI
Throughput Model	DTUs or vCores	Request Units (RU/s)

How do I handle disaster recovery in Azure?

- Implement **geo-redundancy**: GRS for Storage, Active Geo-replication for SQL, zone-redundant services
- Use **Azure Site Recovery** to replicate and failover VMs or physical servers
- Store **backups** in **Recovery Services Vaults**
- Test DR drills periodically

Can I integrate Azure with on-premise systems?

Yes, Azure supports hybrid cloud via:

- **Azure Arc**: Manage on-prem Kubernetes, servers, databases
- **ExpressRoute**: Private network connectivity
- **VPN Gateway**: Encrypted tunnels via public internet
- **Azure File Sync**: Cloud backup of file servers
- **Data Box**: Physical device for bulk transfers

Tip: Use **Azure Stack HCI** to run Azure workloads on-prem.

What is the Well-Architected Framework?

Azure's **Well-Architected Framework (WAF)** provides five pillars for building successful cloud solutions:

1. **Reliability**

2. **Security**

3. **Cost** **Optimization**

4. **Operational** **Excellence**

5. **Performance** **Efficiency**

Use the **Azure Well-Architected Review Tool** to evaluate your workloads: https://aka.ms/azreview

---

How do I automate Azure deployments?

Use **Infrastructure as Code (IaC)** tools:

- **Bicep**: Native DSL for Azure (declarative)
- **ARM templates**: JSON-based deployments
- **Terraform**: Multi-cloud and Azure-native support
- **Pulumi**: Code-first approach (TypeScript, Python, etc.)

Sample Bicep Template:

```
resource storage 'Microsoft.Storage/storageAccounts@2022-09-01' = {

  name: 'myuniquestorage'

  location: 'eastus'

  sku: {

    name: 'Standard_LRS'

  }

  kind: 'StorageV2'

  properties: {}

}
```

What are managed identities in Azure?

Managed Identity provides an automatically managed identity for Azure services. It allows secure access to other resources (e.g., Key Vault, SQL) without storing credentials.

Types:

- **System-assigned**: Tied to the lifecycle of the resource

- **User-assigned**: Reusable across multiple resources

Use Case: Allow Azure Function to read secrets from Key Vault using its identity.

What's the difference between VNet peering and VPN Gateway?

- **VNet Peering**: Direct, low-latency connection between VNets in the same or different regions

- **VPN Gateway**: Encrypted tunnel between on-prem and Azure (or between VNets using IPsec)

Tip: Use peering when both VNets are in Azure; use VPN for hybrid scenarios.

What is Azure Lighthouse?

Azure Lighthouse enables **multi-tenant** management. Service providers or MSPs can manage customer environments using delegated resource access and policies, without switching accounts.

Use Cases:

- Centralized monitoring across clients

- Delegated RBAC and governance

- Automated onboarding with ARM/Bicep templates

Conclusion

These frequently asked questions cover a wide range of topics—from architectural decisions and service comparisons to security, scaling, monitoring, and automation. Azure's depth and breadth can be overwhelming, but understanding these key questions will guide you through most day-to-day challenges and design decisions.

Refer back to this section whenever you need clarity, and don't hesitate to explore the Azure documentation, community forums, or engage Microsoft support channels for deeper technical insights. Cloud architecture is a continuous learning journey—and the more you ask, the better you design.

www.ingramcontent.com/pod-product-compliance
Lightning Source LLC
La Vergne TN
LVHW051428050326
832903LV00030BD/2963